[Taryn Hutchison] writes with [...]
her experiences in lands emerging f [...]
imprisonment. She lived in sometimes dismal [...]
flames shoot out of her walls, suffered pick-pocketing, robbery,
and assault . . . and loved her time there, where people were
hungry for the gospel. Embarrassing episodes . . . share the pages
with spiritual triumphs and the trials of daily living.

WORLD magazine, Susan Olasky
November 2008

[We Wait You] is one of the best books I have read in a long
time. . . It is a well-written, transparent memoir . . . Every single
woman who goes to the mission field needs to read this book.
It really is that good.

Dr. Jeff Iorg, President
Golden Gate Baptist Theological Seminary
Author of several books including
The Character of Leadership

Exciting...life-changing...challenging to the eternally-
minded...encouraging to those who long to make a difference
in the world. All this and more can be said of Taryn Hutchison's
account of her mission work in Eastern Europe. By relating her
own journey, Taryn does more than entertain and inform: she
challenges us to examine our own commitment to follow Christ's
leading, wherever it might take us. I strongly recommend *We Wait
You* to anyone who has an interest in global missions—and also to
those who don't. They need to know what they are missing!

Kay Marshall Strom
Author of 34 books including
*Daughters of Hope: Stories of Witness and Courage
in the Face of Persecution*

You won't even need to pack your bags to take this riveting journey behind the former iron curtain with Taryn Hutchison. Her story is true, breathtaking, miraculous, and well worth reading. I know not only because I loved the book but also because I had the privilege of being with her on the journey.

Ney Bailey
Author, Speaker
Campus Crusade for Christ International

Taryn Hutchison is a fresh voice of those who continue to break new ground telling the old story. . . What Elisabeth Elliot's writing accomplished a generation ago in opening the eyes of the world to tribal missions, Taryn Hutchison skillfully accomplishes in opening the eyes of the world today to global missions. . . You will find yourself laughing and crying at the candid expression of God's warming grace and provision in a gray world of empty shelves that exists no longer in Eastern Europe. Within the covers of this book are run-ins with the Russian mafia, joyous celebrations in the street, intrigue, hidden microphones, faith, and adventure lived out by Taryn and her sea of friends who said "Yes" to God. Woven through the subtext of the book is a hope-filled love story that only God could orchestrate. . . *We Wait You* is a "must-read" not only for short-term mission teams, missionaries and their supporters, but also for every person who desires to live missionally and make an impact for the kingdom of God.

Dr. Eric Swanson
Leadership Network
Co-author of several books including
The Externally Focused Church

It's refreshing to read a book . . . about real people doing real missions with real struggles and accomplishments. . . . The book is spiritual, genuine, and practical.

Dr. Eddie Pate
Chairman of Intercultural Studies Department
and Professor of Missions
Golden Gate Baptist Theological Seminary

We Wait You . . . a fascinating account of one woman's experiences in Romania shortly after Communism fell. You're guaranteed to gain a broader understanding of the oppression under which the Romanian people lived for years, and of the hope they gained through the Gospel.

Grace Fox
Author of several books including the series
10-Minute Time Outs for Women

We Wait You

We Wait You

WAITING ON GOD IN EASTERN EUROPE

TARYN R. HUTCHISON

PW | Pleasant Word
A Division of WinePress Group

ISBN 13: 978-1-4141-1174-2
ISBN 10: 1-4141-1174-6
Library of Congress Catalog Card Number: 2008900195

To Steve

Without you, this book would only be in my dreams.

CONTENTS

EASTERN EUROPE IN 1990

ACKNOWLEDGMENTS

MY FIRST TEAM in Eastern Europe—Bill, Dan, and Vicki—thanks for making me laugh and bearing with me. This is your story too. Vicki, I'm proud of you for being a survivor—of me as a roommate and of cancer.

The others in Bucharest, Daniel and Marian, Mark and Wendy, John and Ann, Nita—and in Cluj, David and Susan, Suzy, Kelly, Melynda—I love you all, and I miss those days of adventure together.

The leadership women throughout the area—Sue, Gwen, Melanie, Kasia, Daniela, Krystyna, Jennifer, Slavica, Oksana, Velislava, Nikki, Cyd, Gordana, Mary, Anya, and Andrea—thanks for the joy of rubbing shoulders with you and so many unnamed others. That week in Lake Bled will always be one of my fondest memories.

Dear Ney, one of the greatest privileges of my life was soaking up your pearls of wisdom as we traveled together. Thank you for inspiring me.

My friends with Campus Crusade, I loved attempting big things for God with you. I will always be one with you in my heart.

We Wait You

My ministry partners, you kept me going and it was truly a team effort all those years. I deeply appreciate your sacrifice and commitment to me.

My friends at Golden Gate Seminary, thanks for encouraging me in this project and sharing a passion for Christ and for the lost.

Kay Strom, my writing mentor who taught me so much more than writing, I am indebted to you for paying it forward.

Loren, Kurt, Steve, and my mentoring group at Mount Hermon, thanks for reading this manuscript and giving me your honest feedback.

Herb, I appreciate your willingness and expertise with the photos.

And then there's my family. Mom, thank you for imparting to me your love of writing, appetite for reading, and a small fraction of your talent. Dad, whatever I attempted, you always applauded me and made me believe I could do anything. Thank you both for trusting that God would take care of me as I followed Him to Eastern Europe.

Kurt, you are the best big brother in the world. For years, I have proudly watched you follow Christ, even as that took you into the heart of the USSR during days much riskier than mine.

My husband, Steve, thank you for believing in me and this book when I had my doubts. You eagerly sacrificed to see this finished, and I love you for that and so much more. I am so glad you waited for me.

And thank you to the Lord of my life, through whom all things are possible.

Looking upon them, Jesus said,
"With men it is impossible, but not with God;
for all things are possible with God."

—Mark 10:27

PROLOGUE:
HOME AT LAST

October 2005, Bucharest, Romania

WE STEPPED DOWN from our train in the Bucharest North station, the same spot where I had arrived 15 years earlier. This time I did not come single. My husband, Steve, stood next to me. It had been five years since I left Eastern Europe, and it felt good to be home at last.

It didn't look like the same place. The station appeared well-lit, and almost clean. No beggars or taxi drivers accosted us. I noticed cafés named Coffee Right and Mac Dan where kiosks had once existed.

My friend Melynda waited for us at the end of the platform. She crammed us and our things into her car and sped through the streets of the capital city. We chattered away, catching up on several years—another baby for her and a husband for me. I tried to absorb every sight and sound and smell. It was all new for Steve.

The number of cars had increased, with horns that worked quite well. New traffic lights, hotels, supermarkets, even a mall with a large movie marquee seemed out of place in the Bucharest

I remembered. Melynda pointed out the long-overdue statues and plaques, commemorating the martyrs from the 1989 revolution. A clock in the city center counted down the days until Romania would become part of the European Union, slated for January 2007. The clock read 455 days.

Only one block from the main boulevard, it looked as if nothing had changed. Melynda drove us through rutted roads to the flat where we would stay. Our building stood in the midst of rows of high-rise apartment blocks. People still squatted along the roadside, calling out to peddle their wares or sell wrinkled apples. Packs of mangy dogs, their ribs showing, patrolled the streets. Potholes and mud littered the roads. The cars parked on the sidewalk were all the identical Romanian model, the Dacia.

After we unloaded our luggage, Melynda took us to the massive Cora supermarket across from my old flat. The grand opening had been the week before. About 20 people stood in each of the 10 check-out lines. Romanians had not forgotten how to wait patiently. Now they waited in straight lines; before it seemed more like mobs.

We ordered pulled pork sandwiches and cola light from Springtime, a fast food place inside the grocery store. I used to dream of the day diet coke would come to Romania. We ordered our food in one line, paid in another, and picked it up in a third line.

"There is no cola light. You can have coke," the server told me after I made it to the last line.

I saw that bottled water cost the same price. "I'll take that instead," I said.

"No, that is not possible. You must have the coke."

"But I don't want the coke."

Melynda tried to convince him. He seemed determined that I could have the coke or nothing. I couldn't get my money back. Steve watched in astonishment.

"I guess some things will never change," I said.

Melynda laughed. "Welcome home, Taryn!"

The next morning, I ran out of hot water in the middle of my shower. I had forgotten.

Steve and I sat on the sofa to pray together, committing our day to the Lord. As we prayed, I started to cry. I am not one to cry easily.

"What's wrong, Sweetheart?" Steve asked.

"It's Romania. I'm back in Romania." Until that moment, I hadn't allowed myself to feel how much I had missed Romania. Now I could not contain my emotions.

I splashed cold water on my face, and Steve and I headed to the Campus Crusade office. As we entered the metro station to go underground, a warm blast of stale air bombarded me, the smell that meant Romania to me. Bodies packed against each other in the metro car. We didn't need to hang on; it was impossible to fall.

All of the staff members serving in the city of Bucharest had assembled at the office for their monthly day of prayer. We were ushered into the room.

Laurenţiu and Clara saw me first. They jumped to their feet and kissed me on both cheeks. Costi waved hello, Marta smiled at me, and John handed me a microphone to greet the staff.

Fifteen years ago, nine Americans had comprised the team, five long-term and four short-term. I stood amazed, looking at a room filled with about 90 staff members. Only three Americans remained. The rest were Romanian nationals. I recognized Monica, Ionel, Sorina, Radu, Anca, Dan. I knew each of their stories. I remembered when they first decided to become followers of Christ as university students. All these years later, they remained faithful.

"It is such a great joy for me to be here today." My words came out rusty in the Romanian language. Still, they poured out of me, along with my tears. "I left part of my heart behind when I left Romania. I love Romania, and I love all of you. The hardest thing I have ever done was to return to the States. But when I did, God brought my friend Steve back into my life to become my husband. Steve is God's gift to me. He is a wonderful husband, but he could not understand me completely. He did not know the places and people that are in my heart. Today, for the first time, the people I love can meet each other. Today I feel whole."

As I sat down, the room erupted with applause. Many of the Romanians cried along with me as I spoke. In spite of my grammatical mistakes, they understood. My heart communicated to them that day.

Our efforts had not been in vain back in 1990. There was nothing extraordinary about my team. God had used us regular people to bear fruit, and much of that fruit had remained and multiplied. Many of our students had gone on to have fruitful ministries as doctors, teachers, or in the business world. Still more had joined Campus Crusade for Christ staff and were serving in other cities in Romania, other countries, even other continents. We had prayed for these dear ones, loved them, talked to them about Christ, and tried to show them Jesus by our lives. We made lots of mistakes, but God stood bigger.

God had provided everything I needed to make it in a world vastly different from my own. Even now, in my ordinary life back "home" in the States, a place that no longer fits well, He gives me grace to trust Him to live without the adrenaline rush. After all, if I can't shine in the present unseen moments, the triumphs of the past don't count for much.

I watched the Romanian staff embrace Steve, and I knew he was beginning to understand the spell that Eastern Europe had cast on me. He told me that he had never been prouder of me. Yes, I felt complete at last.

Chapter 1

PURPLE FLOWERS
IN A DARK PLACE

"Look among the nations! Observe! Be astonished! Wonder!
Because I am doing something in your days—
you would not believe if you were told."

—Habakkuk 1:5

September 1990, Vienna, Austria

"TARYN, YOU'LL BE going to Romania."

Nita's words sounded so matter-of-fact. I had just arrived at the hostel in Vienna for a briefing conference, and Nita had come to personally deliver my assignment. She proceeded to tell me how much she loved Romania and felt certain I would, too. I didn't believe her.

The first two hours of my yearlong mission experience had not started well. If this indicated the kind of year that would follow, I was in trouble.

Just the day before, I had to feign sadness when I said good-bye to my parents at the airport in Philadelphia. Instead, I felt sheer excitement about the adventure before me. I knew I would be spending the year in Eastern Europe, but I didn't know

1

any specifics, only that I could end up in any of five countries. This unknown element added to my thrill.

Romania was known to have the most heavy-handed regime and spartan living conditions of the Soviet Bloc. Spies lurked on every corner, and the people didn't have much water or food. Since I'd prefer a spa weekend to camping any day, I didn't think that would be a good fit for me. However, when I had been asked on the phone if I'd be open to Romania, I had admitted it wouldn't be my first choice, but I'd be willing. Years earlier I had learned to never say "no" to God. I hoped He would see my obedience and reward me for it.

Every day after that phone call, I prayed and I pleaded, "Oh, God, please don't let it be Romania. Please, let me go to Yugoslavia, Czechoslovakia, anywhere but Romania!"

When I checked in at the hostel in Vienna, the desk clerk told me my room was on the next floor up.

"Take the lift," she said. "Your baggage is too heavy for the stairs."

I climbed aboard the elevator, eager to freshen up after the all-night flight, but it didn't budge. So I pushed the button again and again. It still didn't move. As I was about to climb out, someone else entered and manually closed the inner accordion doors, starting the lift on its slow ascent. I had pushed the button marked "2," hoping for the next level, but that level turned out to be "1." My lift creaked on, overshooting my floor. I had forgotten about ground floors in Europe.

I trudged back down the narrow stairs, lugging my bags, and coaxed the key to open my door. The bathroom was my next challenge. The water faucets worked differently, but at least they had water in Austria. I tried to figure out what the contraption was that looked like a urinal as I hunted for the pull-chain to flush the toilet.

I took a deep breath. *OK, I may not be a camper, but I know I can handle these things. Once I get to Poland, or maybe Hungary, if God wills it, I'll—*

That's when Nita knocked on my door with the news about Romania.

I must have given all the right responses while Nita stood there. But as soon as she left, I crumpled to the floor like a limp pile of spaghetti, while scenes from spy thrillers danced in my head. I wondered how I could possibly handle living in a place like Romania if I couldn't even navigate a hostel in Austria.

It's not that I intentionally got on my knees to pray. I wish I'd thought of the symbolism of starting my year by humbly expressing my utter dependence before God. I fell to the floor because I could not stand. I simply did not have any strength in my legs.

From my position of weakness, I cried out to God. "Father, help me! There is absolutely nothing in me that can do what You're asking me to do. I'm going to need You like I've never needed You before. Please, give me the strength and the grace that I'll need every single day to make it in Romania. Please, Lord. I'm depending on You."

Later, as I headed to the opening meeting of the conference, a dark voice hissed at me in my thoughts. *You've made the biggest mistake of your life. Don't be so stubborn.* The voice knew my weakness. *Just admit you made a mistake, go back to the airport, and go home.*

I had learned to dismiss that voice. "No, I'm certain that I am exactly where God wants me to be." I'm not sure if I just thought those words or spoke them out loud.

That evening, I met my team—Bill, Dan, and Vicki. After the meeting, jet lag and all, we took a tram to a Viennese café to get acquainted. As we each described what had happened in our lives to bring us to Eastern Europe, I realized that soon these three strangers would know me better than almost anyone.

We Wait You

What I remember most about our first evening together is that we laughed. We laughed so loudly, in fact, that a refined Austrian woman raised an eyebrow in our direction and sighed. I realized we would have a good team. We would have fun together. Our very survival might hang on whether we took life too seriously or could manage a sense of humor.

The day we met—riding a tram in Vienna (L–R: Dan, Taryn, Bill, Vicki).

That whole week in the grand city of Vienna passed by as a blur to me. Every day, I digested new information and processed new emotions. I heard about the drought in Romania, read that there were five rats to every one person in Bucharest, and bought loads of canned food, because we wouldn't find any there. It all seemed worse than my darkest imaginings.

I kept asking the ones who lived there, "Is there anything pretty in Bucharest?" I am an artist, and I love beauty.

"No, Taryn." They shook their heads emphatically. "There's no beauty at all."

I took that news hard.

4

From Vienna, we made final phone calls to family back home and had sweet prayer times with new friends and old on the other teams going out all over Eastern Europe. We listened to astounding firsthand stories about the miracle of the recent revolutions in each country.

As much as I struggled with the idea of living in Romania, I had to admit to myself that what had just happened there thrilled me in a way nothing had before. I couldn't forget how I felt, just one year earlier, as country after country in Eastern Europe became free. As I had watched scenes on the news of the Romanian Revolution, my heart felt strangely stirred. I had never given a thought to Romania before.

One Year Earlier, Berkeley, California

The fall semester of 1989 kicked off my final year on staff with Campus Crusade for Christ at the University of California at Berkeley. I had already served 10 years at several college campuses sprinkled across the U.S. God had started beckoning me to Eastern Europe a few years before, during a summer project in Yugoslavia that changed the course of my life. Ever since that summer, I'd been preparing to return, just waiting until the right time to leave Berkeley. That time had come. I received an early acceptance for a yearlong project, called Stint for Short-Term International, beginning the following school year.

That is when the impossible began to happen. Communism started falling like dominoes in Eastern Europe. Poland led the way. The day after the Tiananmen Square revolt was quashed in China, on June 4, 1989, Lech Wałęsa led his Solidarity union to victory. By September, Poland had a new non-Communist government, the first of its kind in Eastern Europe.

I never imagined that Gorbachev's reforms, *perestroika* and *glasnost,* would actually work, but Poland had always been different. The Communist regime could never quite get the upper hand with the Catholic Church. After all, the pope was Polish. Communism could not possibly collapse in any of the other Soviet Bloc countries.

And yet, on the October 23 anniversary of their 1956 uprising, newspapers everywhere shouted that Hungary had become free. The world had watched Ronald Reagan stand in Berlin and say, "Mr. Gorbachev, tear down this wall!" Beyond all belief, the East Germans did just that. They demolished the Berlin Wall on November 9, 1989. The images of jubilant East Germans dancing in the streets are forever imprinted on my mind. It didn't end there. Later in November, Czechoslovakia staged the Velvet Revolution and Bulgaria instigated a coup.

The world was changing so quickly, the West couldn't comprehend, the East couldn't adjust, and I couldn't take it in. The Cold War had been a reality my entire life. I was born on the very day that Soviet tanks rolled in to squelch the short-lived freedom in Budapest, Hungary. My generation grew up watching spy movies and Olympic judges who voted according to whether the skater came from the East or the West. By rote, I recited the words that God could do the impossible, but I guess I never really believed I'd live to see it.

The week before Christmas 1989, as homes across America watched *Rudolph, the Red-Nosed Reindeer*, the most amazing thing happened. Romanians rebelled against their dictator, Nicolae Ceaușescu, and the Romanians won. I felt hypnotized by the television news that week, unable to pull myself away. God planted a seed in my heart that soon began to sprout. A love for the Romanian people started to germinate deep inside me.

Unlike the other countries with peaceable exchanges of power, the revolution in Romania involved bloodshed. Hundreds of people lost their lives for the sake of freedom. Romanians had the most evil dictator of the bunch and were the most oppressed, often described as fearful and beaten down. How in the world did they ever get the courage to stand up and fight?

Shortly after Christmas, I listened to a cassette tape translated by a Romanian expatriate, Flory. It presented another side to the story, one I hadn't seen on the U.S. news. Flory's relatives in Romania made the tape, reliving the events of that fateful week. It all started in Timişoara, a border city, on December 15, the date set for the militia to force a Hungarian pastor, László Tökés, into exile. Believers of both Romanian and Hungarian descent made a human chain around his apartment block, stopping the eviction. Fighting soon erupted, raging on for days as believers secretly huddled together in darkened rooms, praying around the clock.

"We were so weary, we did not think we could continue to pray," said a woman's voice on the tape. "The same day we said that was the day the news broke in the West."

The prayer baton had been passed. I picked up that baton, like so many others.

On the tape, I learned that from the beginning, the people chanted, *"Exista Dumnezeu!"* as their rallying cry. God exists! Their quest for freedom was always about God. It involved much more than a political exchange of power. The people were fighting a regime that had indoctrinated two generations of their people that there is no God. They were now joining their voices to let it be known that they didn't believe the government's lies.

God heard them and He moved. He set them free. He broke through the bars of iron holding them captive. The fighting moved to Bucharest. On December 22, 1989, in the old city square, the army dramatically turned. The tanks that had been gunning down unarmed innocent people suddenly made an about-face and aimed their weapons at the *Securitate*, the Secret Police. Ceauşescu, deluded into believing the people adored him, stood on the balcony of the Parliament building to address the crowd. He fled through underground tunnels, then by helicopter to one of his palaces after another in an attempt to elude his

7

pursuers. He and his wife, Elena, were captured, given a speedy trial, and executed on Christmas Day.

September 1990, en route to Bucharest, Romania

The briefing conference had ended. Our train journey to Romania had begun in Vienna, the city of Old World charm and gentility. There were 10 of us traveling together, all single. The veteran team, in our shoes a year earlier, escorted my team of four. They had agreed to stay on another month to help us acclimate, before returning to the States.

Our first stop was Budapest, Hungary. The short trip only lasted three hours, but it seemed as if we were hurtled backward in time, crossing the invisible barrier between the West and the East. Guard towers, now empty, stood on the Hungarian side.

We had all day to explore the exquisite Hungarian capital. The oppressive severity of the Communist regime couldn't extinguish the beauty of this jewel on the Danube. The cold forms of Marx and Lenin towered impassively over the city, silent sentinels to make sure the people followed the rules.

Before boarding our train to continue on to Romania, we bought more food, fearful there would not be enough to ration out until Christmas, when we'd go to the West and stock up again. We stuffed even more cans into our already bulging duffel bags.

One of the few McDonald's existing behind the Iron Curtain stood inside the *Nyugati* (West) train station. We were told it was something of a tradition for Americans to fill up there before the journey to deprivation. This McDonald's had arched domes and chandeliers. I had never seen such an opulent fast food restaurant before. The veteran team relished their cheeseburgers, some devouring them as if they hadn't eaten for days, others slowly savoring each small bite. I wondered how long it would take me to become this starved for a taste of Americana.

8

Once on the train, the 10 of us settled into our berths in two adjacent cabins for our 20-hour, overnight trip. I didn't sleep well; the excitement and newness kept my mind racing.

The Hungarian officials startled us awake at the border, gruffly demanding our passports. As soon as I dozed off again, the Romanian officers slammed the door open and entered with their dogs sniffing and growling. One officer came back with our documents, granting three-month tourist visas for the four of us newcomers, to hold us over until we received our student visas. We had expected a two-week pass.

"This is too much. This is too good for you," the officer said, as he handed us our passports.

I smiled to myself. I knew a secret. God is too good for me.

As the new day dawned, I could see that Romania was more than a step down from Hungary. It seemed I had fallen headfirst into an abyss, descending farther away from America than I'd ever imagined. I sat glued to the grimy window all day, as we chugged along through the Transylvanian Alps. Hints of brilliant autumn colors were beginning to break out. I gazed at pastoral scenes of shepherds leading their flocks and of horse-drawn carts, laden with mounds of hay, trudging along dirt village roads. The Romanian countryside mesmerized me with its beauty. It looked as though it couldn't possibly be any later than 1900. No telephone poles, no billboards, and few cars were visible.

The first thing I remember about Bucharest is how very dark it was. Our train squealed to its stopping place inside the cold, concrete station. There were no lights. We tentatively stepped down. Sweaty young Romanian men in ragged clothes, eager to make a few lei by carrying our bags, greeted us.

Two teenage boys loaded our many bags onto a wooden cart and pulled the cart by thick ropes tied around their necks. Their muscles bulged. It was a job for a pair of oxen. They strained to get the cart through *Gara de Nord* (North station) and onto the street.

My senses were bombarded. Everything seemed so strange and new. I didn't feel afraid, because I trusted the seasoned team. I just let them lead the way, trying to take it all in.

We followed the guys with the cart outside. This was my first view of Bucharest, and I strained to see something in the dusky twilight. There were no streetlights. The guys filled several waiting taxis with our bags.

My taxi looked battered like all the others. The driver, a diminutive man with a tall hat made of curly fleece, opened all four doors, gallantly bowing with a sweeping gesture for us to get in. The pungent smell of cigarette smoke, mixed with his body odor, permeated the small car. He had two pictures dangling from the rear view mirror like fuzzy dice—the Virgin Mary and a topless woman.

He smiled, exposing the few teeth he had, and offered us some French-looking bread in a canvas satchel. The bread reeked of gasoline, but I knew to accept it. I experienced the essence of the Romanian character, hospitality, for the first time in that taxi.

Racing through the empty streets, we bounced over cobblestones and plunged into potholes. We did not have seat belts. People dressed in dark clothing, bowed down and plodding along, became visible just in time for our driver to swerve up on the sidewalk, honking his horn, barely missing them each time.

In a few minutes, the driver brought us to the dorm where I would live for the next year. Darkness veiled the bleak façade. We walked up the steps into a dim lobby and dumped our bags into the elevator that had stopped at the level of our knees. One of the guys climbed in the lift to ride up with our bags, and the rest of us clumped upstairs.

It was hard to keep our balance on the bumpy concrete steps; some tilted downhill, some up. We edged up eight flights, in utter darkness, then felt our way along a pitch-black hallway, feeling the numbers above the doors as if they were in Braille. When we reached 808, we were home.

Vicki and I were exhausted from the journey. We would stay with Shandra and Cheryl for the month, and then their room would become ours when they left. That first night, we spread beach towels on the concrete floor to try to make some sort of padding. It didn't matter how hard my bed felt. Sleep came quickly to my weary body.

I woke up the next morning to Shandra's voice coming from the hallway. "Yes, the new girls are here. They're still asleep, right on the spot where the guys clubbed the rat to death last week."

I bolted to my feet. "I will not sleep on rat guts!" I said. "I'll sleep standing up for the next month if I have to, but I refuse to sleep on rat guts!"

Vicki and I decided to take a walk that morning, to pray and explore our surroundings in the daylight. I studied our dorm from outside. All the buildings around us looked the same. We were lost in a forest of tall concrete structures with no redeeming features. Rusty cranes lined up on rooftops, mute witnesses to projects begun and not completed. These cranes silently testified that Communism had not succeeded.

A flag waved proudly from the end of one of the cranes, the only color I could see. It had three bold stripes of blue, yellow, and red with a round hole in the center of it. The Communist coat of arms had been cut out. I had seen pictures of the old flag, with a red star on top, the sun shining down on Romania, and wheat encircling the idyllic scene. That flag no longer existed.

After walking a few blocks, Vicki and I came to an ornate iron gate, ajar, with green branches poking through the grillwork. We peeked in. Hidden inside, there appeared to be a secret garden. We cautiously pushed the gate open and tiptoed in. The bench-lined stone path led to a pond with lily pads, surrounded by flowers and trees. Steam rose from the surface of the pond. Its beauty took my breath away.

A woman, dressed very properly in an old but well-cared-for wool suit, wearing a hat and high-heeled shoes, strolled toward us on the path.

I approached her with a smile. "Pardon." I used the international word, trying my best to pronounce it the French way. "Do you speak English?"

"A leetle." She came closer.

"Can we," I motioned back and forth between Vicki and myself, "be here?" I spread my arms to encompass the garden, hoping the universal charades language would help her understand. "Is it OK for us?"

"Da." The woman nodded. "Is free garden. *Gradina Botanica*." She pronounced her words carefully. "Yes. Botanical Garden. Is OK for you. You are American?"

"Yes, we are."

"We wait you. Long time. I go now. Good-bye."

Her heels clipped on the cobblestones as she left through the gate we'd just entered.

My heart sang. There was beauty in Romania after all. I tucked away a hope of this garden becoming my special place, the geography of my soul's oasis. I envisioned the garden as the seasons changed. Closing my eyes, I could see puffy drifts of snow around the lake of crystal ice, pink buds on the trees beckoning the coming of spring, later transformed into rich golden and crimson leaves.

Vicki and I walked a bit and then found a bench on which to sit. There we thanked God for bringing us to Romania safely, taking turns praising Him aloud. We asked Him to provide our very own dorm room so we wouldn't have to keep sleeping on rat guts, on a concrete floor.

We finished praying, and something to the right, a touch of purple out of focus, caught my eye. I blinked. The image sharpened. I gasped, seeing my very favorite deep purple flowering bush from Berkeley, California. I loved everything about these flowers, even their name, the "princess flower." I knew that they only grew in a very particular type of climate. Even 20 miles away from Berkeley, in the microclimates of the San Francisco Bay Area, the princess flower didn't flourish. Yet thousands of miles away, this bush thrived in Bucharest, Romania.

As my eyes brimmed full, the Lover of my soul whispered tenderly to my heart: *My child, I will prove worthy of your trust.*

His smile warmed me. In that moment of profound intimacy, I knew that God loved me and would take care of me. After all, He had brought my beloved purple flower all the way to Romania just for my pleasure. I didn't need it. I'd probably survive without drinking in the lovely violet color and touching the soft petals. God gave me something beautiful to delight in, a mark of His deep love for me. If He could do that, I knew He could take care of everything else.

That day in the garden, I believed that He would answer my prayer of utter desperation from the heap on the floor in Vienna, my plea for grace and strength for each new day. But I still wasn't convinced that I could do my part to keep trusting Him to provide.

I had so many doubts about myself. I didn't know what I would do if life really got tough or how I would handle winter in Romania. My biggest concern was if my team would still like me when they saw the real me.

When Vicki and I returned to the Foreign Students' Dorm, we met an Israeli man on the steps and chatted with him. He told us he had grown up in Bucharest, and his family had fled during World War II. He was so proud that his daughter Orna was now a student at the university in his home country. We told him we were here to learn the Romanian language as the preparatory year for our university studies. After a few minutes of conversation, he wished us *"Shalom!"* and started walking away.

We watched as he turned and began to walk back toward us. "I vas t'inking," he said. "Today, my daughter, she move out of dormitory. Do you need place to live?"

We moved our suitcases to Orna's room, number 507, within the hour. Vicki, a petite blonde from Texas, with an unassuming manner, had packed more than the rest of us. Dan quickly came to her assistance, claiming her suitcases weighed more than she did. Vicki's luggage proved to be too much for one guy, so Bill had to help. I, on the other hand, hauled my own bags; glad we were moving downstairs, not up.

That night, Vicki and I recounted our first full day as we lay in our beds, side by side. We thanked God for what He had done for us. He had given us a dorm room so we wouldn't have to sleep on concrete any longer. He had given me purple flowers to enjoy.

My mind spilled over with everything that had changed in my life during the past week. For a long while after Vicki's breathing had slowed to the point of sleep, I continued to ponder the events. I wondered what the next days would hold. *Would I remember this day? Would this sweet intimacy be enough to sustain me? Would I always feel this close to God?*

Sleep evaded me as the noise from a party next door intensified. Our neighbors, male medical students from Greece, belted out what I guessed were Greek drinking tunes with a finalé of shattering glass. Their loud words were slurred. They were wasted.

My annoyance turned to terror as I watched shadowy forms crawl over onto our balcony, six flights above the ground. The party had moved to our room. My blood froze. Soundlessly, I put on my glasses and shoes. I nudged Vicki, still sleeping peacefully, whispering to her to do the same. We had to be ready.

Orna had stacked her furniture, which we now owned, neatly on the tiny balcony. The two guys, wearing only their underwear, threw it piece by piece over the railing, sending it splintering to the ground. Their raucous laughter, as each piece of furniture crashed, reverberated in my ears.

When our balcony doorknob started to turn, Vicki and I got up silently and crept toward our hallway door to dash to safety. Just then, someone called to the Greek men. They turned around and climbed back to their own balcony.

We were safe. It took several minutes for my pulse to acknowledge this.

Vicki and I whispered our thanks to God for watching over us.

Thus ended the morning and the evening, the first day. My first full day in Romania had come to a close, the first of many days that I would watch, utterly amazed, God's provision and His protection in a land far from home.

What About You?

- You don't need to be on the other side of the world to experience God's provision. What situations are you facing that are beyond you—where you have to depend on God's strength and grace?

- Describe an unexpected blessing God has given you, like the purple flowers, purely to show how much He loves you.

- Recount times you have watched in amazement as news events unfolded that seemed impossible—even for God.

Chapter 2

FREEDOM!

*"I will go before you and make the rough places smooth;
I will shatter the doors of bronze, and cut through
their iron bars."*

—Isaiah 45:2

October 1990, Bucharest, Romania

I FELT NERVOUS. I stood in the hallway with my team, waiting to be called into the English classroom where I would give a lecture. None of the teams before us had ever attempted anything this big. We had only been in-country for a month and in language class just two weeks. I planned to speak on two forbidden subjects that day—democracy and Jesus Christ.

I could not get the nightmare out of my mind. It seemed so real. I was in the middle of presenting my talk, when the *Securitate* burst into the room, machine guns pointed, yelling loudly. Students screamed and threw themselves on the floor. The officers blindfolded Bill, Dan, Vicki, and me, then tied our wrists behind our backs. We were presented our last (and first) cigarettes, then shoved to face the wall. Bill was shot first. As he lay writhing on the floor, Dan was executed, then Vicki. My turn had come when I suddenly woke up, sweating.

I had good reason to be nervous. No one knew if Romania was really free. The new leader, Ion Iliescu, had been Ceauşescu's right-hand man. "Former" Communists comprised the ruling FSN party, National Salvation Front. There was even talk that the revolution had been set-up.

Romanians were still suspicious of everyone, even family members. They had been brainwashed that one out of every four Romanians were spies, part of the *Securitate*. The government had maintained tight control over the people through fear and intimidation. Trust did not return overnight.

And then there were the events of a few months ago. Beginning in April, only four months after the revolution, university students were striking, protesting the new regime's policies and chanting, "Down with Communism!" Iliescu called the students *golani*, meaning rascals. On June 14, 1990, he brought in over 10,000 miners to Bucharest by special trains. The government called on the allegiance owed by the miners, such as the obligation workers in the States might feel for their union.

As the armed miners converged, students fled to barricade themselves inside the university buildings. Many were beaten and killed. Estimates on the exact number of golani martyrs are unclear, but many guessed it ran into the hundreds. Graffiti on the plaza where the murders occurred renamed it *Piaţa Tiananmen II*. Iliescu later claimed that he had sent the miners to Bucharest to plant pansies.

Some students invited me to view a homemade documentary film about this horror in an old downtown cinema. The girls whispered translation into my ear, but the images I saw didn't need to be interpreted. After about 20 minutes, officers stormed in to the theater, yanked the film out of the projector, and ordered everyone to leave. Romania was not yet free.

18

It had only been a few days since I first met Profesoara Popa in the Filologie Faculty (Languages Department). She was the chief of that department. I introduced myself and offered my help. If she would like a native English speaker to address her classes, I would be happy to do that.

"An American! So, you have come at last. We wait you for 45 years. You never come. Tell me, what is an American doing in my country now?" She studied me carefully.

My answer had been well-rehearsed. "I am a student in the History of Art faculty. Now I am in my preparatory year of Romanian language, and after that is finished, I will study my favorite sculptor, Constantin Brâncuși." The paperwork was being legally processed to allow us to be in Romania as missionaries. In the meantime, we were students who just happened to be believers, naturally wanting to tell our new friends about our personal faith.

"You know Brâncuși?" Her eyes sparkled.

"Oh, yes. I studied him in the States, and I greatly appreciate his work."

Romanians were proud of their famous son. From the moment I first saw his sculptures in the Philadelphia Museum of Art, I was enthralled. An abstract sculptor working in Paris in the first half of the twentieth century, he had been significantly influenced by the simplified shapes and clean lines of African art. I truly loved his work, and was still amazed at the instant rapport this connection gave me with Romanians.

At that meeting, Profesoara Popa invited me to speak in English to every classroom in her department. That meant we would have access to 4,000 students. I floated home from my appointment.

I didn't have much time to get ready for this English lecture. After language class one day, I took the tram to the American Consulate library to research some facts about democracy, the topic Profesoara Popa had chosen without hesitation.

The day before the lecture, as I stressed about how unprepared I felt, God reminded me not to worry. I put my notes away and chose to spend time reading His Word and praying instead. My reading that day was in Luke 21, where Jesus spoke about the certainty of being persecuted in the end times. His words related perfectly to my situation. I felt as if He had spoken them just for me, just for this time.

"It will lead to an opportunity for your testimony," I read in verses 13–15. "So make up your minds not to prepare beforehand to defend yourselves; for I will give you utterance and wisdom which none of your opponents will be able to resist or refute."

My heart felt calmed. I realized again that I simply had to trust that God was in control, and that He'd put His words in my mouth. I prayed that students would see Jesus in our speech and demeanor, and that they would not be able to resist Him.

Profesoara Popa opened the door and called the four of us to enter her classroom. A wooden platform stood at the front of the room. Every professor in the Filologie Faculty sat on the stage, looking quite stiff with their proper suits. I was unprepared to see the four who team-taught our Romanian language class. They were going to be wise to us now. They might guess our real reason for being in Romania. My pulse quickened. Now I had another reason to be tense.

Profesoara Popa formally introduced the four of us to the class. Bill, Dan, and Vicki were ushered to the empty seats on the platform. I stood at the podium, with the entire entourage seated behind me. I faced a classroom of about 150 students, all dark-haired and wearing dark clothes, eager to hear a real American accent, since they learned British pronunciation. I recognized a few of the students we had been getting to know. Mariana and Irina were there, smiling back at me. I spotted

Freedom!

Adrian, the guy who cleaned our blackboards every day. He winked.

I spoke to the class about the birth of democracy, starting with Greek city-states about 590 B.C. I told them that democracy means "rule by the people" and that the constitution of the United States has been in existence, unchanged, longer than any other.

Their faces were attentive but too serious. I didn't feel as though I was connecting with these students personally. My delivery felt unnatural, like a dry monologue.

That's when I heard a noise behind me. "Whoa, whoa, whoa!" By now this was a familiar sound, in Bill's thick Georgia accent.

I turned to see Bill, arms flailing wildly, and his chair tumble off the edge of the platform. With his wrestler's build, he landed on the ample lap of one of our Romanian language teachers, a robust woman named Profesoara Zaharie.

"Pardon. I am so sorry," Bill said.

"It is not a problem." She giggled and good-naturedly squeezed him as someone else righted his chair.

I was horrified. The students, however, enjoyed it. They laughed, and the tension broke. Something about Bill's humility and humor attracted the Romanians. I needed Bill to loosen me up that day, to help me relax. He came through.

When the snickering stopped, I went on to tell the class why I think democracy has worked for America. Our belief in all men being created equal and our system of checks and balances have been good things. I proclaimed to those students with their fledgling democracy that I believe the biggest reason our system has succeeded in America is that our country was founded with an acknowledgment of God's authority, according to His moral code of right and wrong. Even though we sometimes falter, we have His principles to bring us back to the right course.

21

I quickly thought about our Romanian language professors seated behind me, debating whether or not I should go on to say all that I had planned. Taking a deep breath, I decided to go for it. I added that God made His ways known to us by giving His written Word, the Bible, and by sending His Son, Jesus, to show us what He is like. I told them that anyone can know God through a personal relationship with Jesus Christ.

As the question and answer time began, Vicki started passing around a few sheets of paper for the students to write their name and room number if they would like to talk more about Jesus. Vicki was always the helpful one who volunteered to do those behind-the-scenes tasks.

Dan helped me field questions. The no-nonsense guy from Missouri, he was the brain in our group, at least in terms of political science. I felt so thankful to be able to rely on him. I was the public speaker, but he had the knowledge.

When the questions were finished, the students gave me a standing ovation. The professors bowed to us, presented Vicki and me with flowers, and kissed all four of us on both cheeks. Then they whisked us away to a champagne reception that had been prepared to honor us. We entered a stately room with tall ceilings and unlit crystal chandeliers. Faded velvet draperies showcased the floor-to-ceiling windows.

The professors gathered around to speak with each of us. Several claimed that just a few months earlier, they would have been interrogated for hours for merely speaking to a foreigner. They would never have had the courage to say the name of God aloud, fearing they'd lose their jobs or worse. There had been absolutely no mention of God in their country for 45 years. They thanked me for bringing taboo topics into the open.

Most of these *inteligenţia* were born after the Communists took over. Although they were adamant that the state didn't have the right to officially declare that God did not exist, that didn't mean they believed in Him. They simply believed that no subjects should be banned from being spoken about publicly.

I had goose bumps as the professors expressed the wonder of freedom of speech and freedom in education, concepts that I, as a spoiled American, had taken for granted. However, I realized the irony that there were not many classrooms in the United States where a personal relationship with Jesus Christ could be proclaimed as boldly as I had done here.

"We wait you. Why did you take so long?" one professor asked me. I could no longer count the number of times this question had been directed to me since I had arrived in Romania.

"We waited 45 years for the Americans to come and set us free," said another professor.

I had no answer for this. I felt ashamed that the Allies had given Eastern Europe over to the Soviets after the war. General Patton wanted to go on to Moscow after Berlin; he and Churchill had an idea of what would come.

There was no sense of condemnation, however, in the question posed by Romanians. I only heard joy that we were here now, relief that freedom had come to them at last, at least in small steps as they progressed toward true democracy. Whether the revolution had fully succeeded or not, these professors were hopeful. They were finally free of their dictator. That was reason enough to celebrate.

"When I was a child, we used to say that even if the Americans were coming in a wheelbarrow, they should be here by now," one of the women said, laughing.

Each time I took a sip from my champagne flute, I would set it down, and when I picked it up again, there was nothing in it. I saw Dan's puzzled expression as he also picked up an empty glass. This mysteriously happened several times before I spied Bill pouring Vicki's champagne into the potted plants. I wondered if the plants would get a little tipsy that night.

We had a no-drinking policy during our Stint year. At our briefing, we were given an exception. If it would be rude to our hosts to refuse, we were allowed to nurse a drink. As the Associate Team Leader, I thought this was one of those occasions. Obviously Bill, who trumped me as the Team Leader, did not agree.

I noticed the plump professor that Bill had landed on talking to him, giggling and blushing. Her sweet face was framed by brunette hair pulled up in a French twist. Profesoara Popa murmured to me that her name, Zaharie, means sugar. She certainly seemed to fit her name.

Another professor approached to ask if I had read George Orwell's *Animal Farm*. I had. Orwell's story of the animals uprising and taking over the farm mirrored how the Communists had asserted themselves in this part of the world. I recalled that the pigs became the supervisors, the power went to their heads, and they began to steal the other animals' milk and apples for themselves.

He spoke with a perfect British accent. "I wonder, can you recall the most famous line from Orwell's book?"

I thought a moment. "Umm…all animals are equal, but some animals are more equal than others. Is that it?"

"Yes, 'tis correct," he said. "If you want to know about Romania today, you must understand that sentence."

Once we had taken our leave and moved out of eyesight of the academic building, Bill gave me a high-five. "Good job, Sis!"

It was a moment of absolute elation for our team. We jumped and cheered and danced around. Dan told us he'd counted the names on the sign-up sheet.

"We have over 100 students to talk to!"

"God, You're awesome!" Bill said. "Y'all know what, our God is awesome. Let's thank Him right now."

The four of us stopped there in the open. We prayed and sang our worship to God, right out loud for all Romania to hear.

Overcome by emotion, I often had to stop singing. We praised God for what He had done that day, and then we interceded for the people of Romania to not be able to resist the love of Jesus Christ.

Too keyed up to go back to our rooms, we took the metro downtown to find a restaurant. We had been keeping score. We called it the Restaurant Rating Review. Every time we ate out, we each had three points we could award, based on food, service, and ambiance. If there existed a really good restaurant in Bucharest, which we had yet to find, it could receive a top score of 12 points. To date, our highest score totaled three points. The Dunarea (Danube) had been in first place, with five points, until we got home and were all afflicted with a disease similar to the name of the restaurant. We took those five points away.

For this celebration meal, we chose Casa Capşa, empty except for us. The waiter seated us and demanded that we take our coats to the coat check room. It felt as cold inside as out, so I preferred to keep mine on, but he insisted. When we returned, there were four plates of food on our table. The waiter had never brought us menus, because there was only one choice. It was some sort of pork with something like dumplings. Vegetables were rare. We had mineral water with gas, as they called carbonation. Our napkins, one each, were tiny squares, as thin as tracing paper.

The food didn't taste bad, and I liked the worn elegance of the room, imagining it in its prime. Typical for Europe, the waiter didn't interrupt our evening to ask us how we liked the food, if we needed anything else, or to refill our water. When we stood up to claim our coats, he appeared, presenting us with the bill. The total for all four of us equaled eight dollars.

This was our best dining experience yet, the perfect cap to such a memorable day. We cast our votes, and the Capşa moved into first place. It received eight whopping points.

We enjoyed the evening so much that we forgot all about the time. The most important hour of each day was between 8:00 and 9:00 in the evening, when the government turned on the water. We planned our life around the water. Tonight, for the first time, it had slipped by us. And none of us minded.

Usually, Vicki and I had the water hour down to a science. It would spurt out rusty at first; after it cleared, we filled up every container we had. We then poured water into the toilet and flushed it by pulling the rope overhead, the only time each day it got flushed. One of us would go into the kitchen and wash the dishes, warming the water on our lone gas burner. The other one would sit in the tub to bathe with the hand-held shower nozzle. When the water came out hot, which rarely happened, we could fill up the tub and actually soak in it.

This night was filled with events more important than water.

Vicki and I first met Mariana during a break from language class. She sat in the cantina with her roommates, sipping Turkish coffee with her cigarette poised between her fingers. Her dark beauty was striking, her hair cut in a bob.

When she heard us speaking English, her eyes lit up. She exuded a confidence that I hadn't seen in many Romanians.

Mariana turned to face us at the next table. "Please don't be angry with me. Would you mind if I speak English with you?"

We met often those next couple of weeks. Mariana, a typical young Romanian woman, was adept at sewing and cooking and passionate about the arts. It seemed that she could do anything.

One evening, she brought her guitar to our room and sang music she had written, then she recited her poetry. She even wore a sweater she had knit herself. Each time we got together, Vicki and I divulged a little bit more of the mystery of who Jesus is and what He means to us.

The evening after the English lecture, Vicki and I walked to Mariana's room. Ever the hostesses, Mariana and her roommate, Irina, started brewing up some Nescafe for us on the hot plate. Irina took two wrinkled apples, wiped them on her blouse, and handed them to us.

"Please." She nodded.

Mariana pulled out two square wooden stools for us to sit down.

From that vantage point, I surveyed their room. Much smaller than the ones for us foreign students, it didn't have a kitchenette. Rather than two people sharing the room, there were eight. Four bunk beds, with every bed neatly made, encircled the electric hot plate with its frayed cord. We foreigners each had our own bathroom, but here there was one for every six rooms. That added up to 48 girls to a bathroom. The girls told me that they carried their own light bulb to the shower. A friend would guard the bulb, a valuable commodity, while they bathed.

Other roommates began trickling in, returning from their full day of classes. It was their first time to come back to their room since early that morning. Each girl, one after another, went through her daily ritual upon returning from class—first taking off her shoes, polishing them, then neatly lining them up against the wall. After changing to pajamas, they started spot cleaning and mending the clothes they had just removed. Romanians had one outfit they wore to school and one nicer outfit for parties and special occasions. That was it. These clothes had to last a long time, and they did their best to care for them. I felt humbled every time I witnessed this ritual.

Mihaela plopped down on her bunk and started copying a Mathematics textbook. There were only a couple of textbooks for each class. The students took turns, taking the book home overnight to laboriously copy the chapters by hand, in flawless handwriting. The following day, it would be passed on to the next person. It might be their turn to have it again in a month or so.

Mihaela showed me the book. "Have you seen this before? It is a photograph of the brilliant author of all of our academic books." Her voice dripped with sarcasm.

She opened to the front cover. A picture of Elena Ceaușescu stared up at me, wife of the former dictator who had named her the Vice Prime Minister of Romania and touted her as the country's leading scientist. Elena had only finished the fourth grade; Nicolae quit school at age 11. It was laughable that they had paraded as authors of university books. Nicolae had called himself the Genius of the Carpathians. Most of their pictures had been ripped out of the textbooks, just as the Communist symbols had been cut out of the flags. Now I caught a glimpse of history, life before the revolution.

Once the coffees were handed out, everyone found a spot on one of the beds. By this time there were about seven of us in the room.

Mariana looked especially buoyant. Her countenance seemed changed. Her usually bright eyes were lit from the inside this time.

"I thought about our conversations, and I started to read the Bible you gave me. Before I met you both, I have felt empty inside. I knew there had to be something more to life, but I did not know what. My grandmother used to speak of God, but I was taught it was all a fable that only silly old women believed. But lately I have thought that perhaps my grandmother knew something I did not know."

She took a sip of her coffee and continued. "I prayed to God a few months ago, and I said, 'God, please let me know if You are there.' I think you two were sent to me from God as my answer. He is telling me that it is true; He is here. I decided last night that I want to follow Jesus. I prayed to Him and asked Him to come into my life."

Vicki and I jumped up and hugged Mariana. I told her there would never be a more important decision for her to make in her life. We promised to help her learn how to grow in this newfound relationship. It struck me as curious that she wasn't a bit self-conscious to talk about these private issues in front of her roommates. That didn't happen in the States.

I told the girls that I had made a decision like Mariana's when I was 14. "A young couple moved to my village, and I noticed something different about them—something I'd never seen before. I came to understand the difference was their relationship with Jesus. They told me God loves me so much He sent His Son, Jesus, to forgive my sins and give me new life. I knew I needed Jesus, but I was afraid He'd take away all my fun. One night, as I lay in bed thinking about this, I decided to risk it and trust Him with my fears. I gave my life to Jesus that night, and I've never regretted it. And you know, I have had fun, and even something deeper called joy."

The next evening, we heard a rap on our door. Mariana, Irina, and Mihaela were there. This time Irina's face shone from within.

"Last night, I could not sleep." The words bubbled out of her. "My mind was filled of all the things you and Mariana talked about. I got up out of bed and I stood on my knees on floor. I prayed to God, and I said, 'God, I know I need You. I know I am sinner, but I am scared. If You are real, I ask You to come into my life.' I woke up this morning, and I felt different. I felt happy. I wanted to come and tell you this. Does this mean He is in my life? Does it mean He is real?"

"Yes, Irina. That is what it means." Vicki and I congratulated Irina, our eyes glistening along with hers.

Vicki started to explain to Irina and Mariana how they can be certain that Christ is in their lives and that He will never leave. Wanting to be a good Romanian hostess, I offered the girls *ceai*, the Romanian word for chai-tea. I listed the flavors of *ceai* that we had, asking which they would prefer.

"You choose for us," Mariana said.

"How many teaspoons of sugar would you like?"

"Four." The others nodded in agreement.

I went into our tiny one-person kitchen, opening the cupboard where we kept the sugar and tea. It looked like Bill and Dan had found some more sugar today. There was a new baggie filled with it. I took that out, along with cinnamon apple tea bags. After the tea was steeped, I stirred in four teaspoonfuls for our guests and took the teacups out to them. Vicki and I both liked ours plain.

Mihaela took the first sip.

"*De ce?*" Her voice croaked.

I had learned last week that "*de ce*" means "why." I thought she wanted to know why I had chosen cinnamon apple.

"*De ce nu?*" I said, proud of myself for remembering how to say "why not?"

The girls politely finished their tea, taking small sips. Their little fingers were pointed and their lips were pursed, befitting respectable Victorian ladies. I noticed some strange expressions that passed between them. There were still so many things I didn't understand about this culture, I couldn't guess what that meant.

After a shorter than usual visit, the three girls left. Vicki and I promised to come to visit them soon.

We settled down to our language homework, and were interrupted by another knock. This time Mihai and Mircea stood at our door, two of the guys Bill and Dan had befriended.

"We cannot find the guys. Do you know where they are?"

"I'm not sure, but they're supposed to come here in half an hour. Want to wait for them here?"

When they agreed, I decided once again to be a proper Romanian and offered the guys some *ceai*. I stirred in the customary four teaspoonfuls of sugar and handed them the cups.

Mihai took a big gulp. He spit it out. "Are you trying to kill me?"

"What! What are you talking about?"

"You put salt in the tea!"

Mircea held his stomach and laughed. He could do that because he hadn't taken a drink of his tea yet.

I opened up the baggie from Bill and Dan and took a taste. Sure enough, it was salt.

Another secret to understanding the Romanian culture was unlocked for me that evening. The sweet girls politely drained their cups, not wanting to hurt my feelings. The guys, however, were a little less encumbered by the nuances of social etiquette.

I still had so much to learn about Romania, but there was no place on earth that I would rather be. It boggled my mind to think that someone raised on a chicken farm on the Eastern Shore of Maryland now lived in the Soviet Bloc. I taught the meaning of freedom to students stepping out on unsteady legs into democracy, while taking my own shaky steps of faith. As overwhelming as that was, something much more amazing overshadowed it. I witnessed lives being transformed as people found true freedom in Christ, the kind of freedom that will last forever. God Himself had shattered the doors that had once imprisoned these dear ones, and now those doors stood open wide.

What About You?

- How can you take the next step of faith in your journey—maybe it's just a baby step—to move out of your comfort zone and toward God?

- Perhaps you've never made that decision that Mariana and Irina made. Maybe you're just not sure all this is true. Think about this: Has anything dramatic or personal enough ever happened to you to cause you to think there could be a God who is both infinite and personally caring? What is keeping you from taking the first step and asking God to let you know if He is there?

- If you have taken that step already, think of the people whose paths intersect with yours. Now think of ways you can build a relationship with them, hoping to show them Jesus by your life and words.

Chapter 3

GRACE IN THE
DAILY GRIND

*I can do all things through Him who strengthens me....
And my God shall supply all your needs according to
His riches in glory in Christ Jesus.*

—Philippians 4:13,19

October 1990, Bucharest, Romania

MY HONEYMOON PHASE soon began to wear off.
Typically, life in a new country begins with adventure and
discovery, but the reality of everyday life in Romania quickly
replaced that. Golden autumn sunshine succumbed to white
skies as the last leaves drifted to the ground.

Every day echoed the one before. Get up early, sit in language
class for five hours, find food, do homework, talk to students
in the dorms, stay up much too late because of the noise from
the party next door, wake up exhausted to start it all over again.
Some days we added a new twist to the routine and washed out
our clothes by hand, hanging them on the spider's web of rope
we draped from one ceiling pipe to another. I hadn't known
how much muscle strength it took to wring out jeans; I'd never

washed them by hand in the States. Our jeans and towels usually dripped on us for a couple of days before they were dry enough to take down.

Each morning in language class, the teachers asked us to talk about what we did the day before. Our teachers never spoke to us in English. Only one of the four even knew English. Our textbooks were written entirely in Romanian, without any English explanations. We were learning by complete immersion in the language, trying to figure things out by the context.

We each learned language differently and at different speeds. Dan and I were the most willing to take a risk and speak to strangers. Dan had the best handle on grammar; my strength was vocabulary. Vicki needed to have it all sorted out perfectly in her mind before she said anything. Bill struggled with just about every aspect of language learning.

Whenever our teacher would be at her wit's end with Bill, he would do something disarming, such as hand out loaves of bread all around. The teacher would generally sigh, mutter murderous thoughts under her breath, such as "Beel, I keel you," and move on to pronouns.

Eastern Europeans taught by negative reinforcement. They hoped that by humiliating a student, he'd remember the embarrassment and never make the same mistake again.

Dan came in one morning, eager to tell a story in Romanian. "We had flowers in a vase on our table. They had white petals and a yellow center. We call them daisies. OK, *margaretas*. Yesterday when I came home to get lunch, I noticed that Bill had cut the tops off the *margaretas*. Only the stalks were in the vase." He turned to face the culprit. "Bill, why did you do that?"

Vicki translated into Bill's ear what Dan had said. "I didn't do anything," Bill said. "You're the one who did it. When I went into the bathroom, I saw the tops of the daisies laid in a perfect semicircle at the base of the toilet. That's just weird, Dan."

That day, I learned the word for daisy, and I also learned that something mysterious was going on in the guys' room. After class, the four of us had planned to eat lunch together in Bill and Dan's room. Once a week, we opened another can of our rationed tuna from Vienna. While the guys fixed the meal, Vicki and I started on our homework, each sitting cross-legged on one of the twin beds.

Vicki spotted it first. A worm-like tail slithered from underneath her bed to mine. "A mouse!" she screamed. "Taryn, there's a mouse under your bed!"

I jumped to my feet, squealing out a duet with Vicki.

Dan bent down to check it out. "It's a big mouse. I think it's a rat."

Bill sized up the rodent. "Yep, that's a rat, all right."

He and Dan chased the rat as it scampered into the bathroom. It picked up a daisy top in its mouth before escaping into a hole under the bathtub.

"Well girls, I think we might have solved the mystery," Bill said.

I still found it hard to believe that a rat could climb up on the table to chew flowers. But just in case, my appetite for eating tuna sandwiches in the guys' room had fled. We decided to transport the lunch to our place. However, we had to get off the beds and step our feet down on the floor to do this. And neither Vicki nor I were thrilled about that.

The guys brought all four chairs over to the edge of the bed where I stood, making a straight line that extended halfway across the room. Vicki jumped to my bed, and then we both hopped from chair to chair, ending up on the two farthest from the bed. Then the guys moved the empty chairs to the other side of us, and we stepped onto those. Eventually, we were able to land in the hallway, safe at last.

The next morning in language class, I learned a very useful word as we recounted our adventure. *Şobolan* means rat.

That afternoon, it was my turn to "find" food. Romanians don't use the verb "buy" for food, because it can require a rather extensive hunt. Vicki and I had our very own *pungas*, canvas bags which were an essential item in every Romanian woman's purse. If we ever saw something we wanted to buy, we had to be ready, because we never knew if we would see it again.

We knew we needed to get *pungas* the day that Vicki spotted diet cokes at one of the kiosks. She ran home with as many cans as she could carry. By the time we returned with our duffel bag, hoping to fill it up, the diet cokes were gone. We imagined that a case had fallen off a truck, en route from Istanbul to Hungary. We never saw diet cokes again.

The state-run grocery stores overflowed with rows of barren shelves. This particular day, one lone mason jar of tomato paste sat on a shelf. A woman with dyed burgundy hair sat at the cashier's booth, polishing her nails. She seemed angry at my interruption. It wasn't that she was lazy. I wanted to buy something that would pad the government's pocketbook, not hers. I had been told that all employees of the state were paid $30 per month, whether a university professor or a janitor, whether they worked hard or not. They'd rather not. It was perfectly understandable.

Around the corner, an outdoor market called a *piaţa* pulsed with life. Peasants hauled wagonloads of fresh produce into the city while it was still dark, pulled by sturdy work horses. Everything was organic—apples ridden with worm holes, rubbery carrots showing evidence of the earth they'd been pulled from, eggs with feathers and poop attached.

I put a thin five-lei coin (worth less than a penny) in a farmer's leathery hand, noticing the dirt under his nails and ground into his wrinkled skin. He carefully placed 11 eggs in my *punga* and tried to give me two lei in return. I shook my head and closed my hand. He spit out his sunflower seeds and smiled broadly at me with his few teeth.

Without cartons to protect my eggs, I gingerly toddled to the next stall, overflowing with vibrant flowers, riotous color enlivening the *piaţa*. I bought five carnations from a gypsy lady whose brightly patterned skirt and scarf competed with the flowers. In Romania, it is bad luck to buy even numbers of flowers. The woman handed me four more carnations, making the total remain an odd number. I tried to give her more money, but she refused. She pointed to my mouth and made a big smile with hers, pulling up the corners by hand.

"Nice. I like," she said. I realized she offered me free flowers because she liked my smile. This lady lived hand-to-mouth, and yet she gave me flowers. As an American, I was wealthy in comparison to her. I felt overwhelmed by her kindness.

I had to walk through the meat section, my least favorite part, to exit. A petite woman sat next to her basket of live chickens. I guessed her age at about 70 years old. I watched her deftly break a chicken's neck with a single swing like a lasso. Whole sides of cows hung from pegs. The stench overpowered me, and my stomach started to retch involuntarily. It looked as though dark fur covered the cow sides, but as I got closer, walking with my hand held tightly over my nose, I saw instead that the carcasses were shrouded by black flies.

The only stores that seemed to attract business were the bread stores. People would line up for blocks to go inside a *pâine* store. Bread existed as the staple of Romanian life. There was always bread. And it smelled so good baking. Every day we bought just that day's amount of bread. With no preservatives, it would petrify overnight.

That afternoon, I waited in line outside the pâine store closest to our dorm. A woman scurried out of the store. *"Şobolan!"* she cried.

In memorizing a new vocabulary word, it's helpful to hear it used in a real life context right away. Now that I knew what this word meant, I quietly got out of line, along with a handful of people, none of us making a fuss. Most chose to remain in the queue. I couldn't handle bread from a store that had a rat. Not yet anyway.

Sundays in Bucharest were joyful days of rest. Romanians loved to express their newfound freedom of religion. Some attended church out of curiosity. They wanted to understand the faith of their ancestors, most of whom had been Romanian Orthodox.

It's not that all churches were closed under Communism. Priests who touted the party line, praising Our Father Ceauşescu, seemed to be unaffected. Spies planted themselves in congregations of the few Bible-believing churches left open, recording the name of each person who entered. Many of those people mysteriously lost their jobs the next day. Sometimes the outspoken ones simply disappeared, never to be seen again.

I attended one of the persecuted Protestant churches, named Popa Rusu for the street on which it stood. The building was very plain, and hidden between other buildings. Nothing about the exterior marked it as a church.

The interior was a whole different story. People crowded onto each bench, unencumbered with Westerners' need for personal space. The ones who couldn't squeeze onto a bench stood in the aisles, pressed against each other. Hundreds crammed into any space they could find. The windows were closed, because Romanians firmly believed that colds were caught through drafts. The room felt quite warm, but not as warm as the passion of the people.

The depth of faith in that room humbled me. Many of these believers had suffered for years, never faltering in their belief that living for Jesus was more important than anything. They didn't demand that He give them good health, good jobs, money, safety, or freedom—willingly laying all of that aside. Yet they were truly free, even the ones who had been imprisoned, harassed, or had loved ones tortured or murdered because of Christ.

Others in Romania had warded off the despair by clinging to the ember of hope that the Americans would come some day to save them. Some succumbed to the hopelessness, resigned to never escaping their bleak existence, everyday the same. But these dear followers of Christ held firm to the confident hope that Jesus will return for them one day. The change in political system didn't make their faith any stronger; it just gave them more to praise God for. Their joy had no bounds. I had so much to learn from them. They knew how to wait on God.

Trying to be separate from the world, they had some strict practices. Men sat on the left of the sanctuary and women on the right. Married women wore scarves on their heads to symbolize their submission to their husband and to God. None of the women wore jewelry or make-up. I didn't think it was a sin to try to look pretty, but I didn't want to offend anyone. So I scrubbed my face clean and shiny before church. It was a very small sacrifice to make.

One of the first church services I attended was the Thanksgiving service in October. It had nothing to do with Pilgrims or turkeys, but focused on giving thanks to God. As usual, everyone greeted each other by saying *"pace"* or peace.

A young girl, about 12 years old, ran over to me when I entered. Her name was Adriana, and she reminded me of the Romanian gymnasts from the Olympics. "I translate for you," she said. She stuck to me as though attached with velcro.

Vicki and I sat on the women's side, next to Adriana and her mother. One lone man sat on our bench, probably in his eighties. He was blind, and his wife took care of him. I caught his wife's eyes. They positively twinkled.

She stretched her scrawny arm around several people to reach me. That's when I discovered those arms were far from weak. She grabbed my neck and pulled me over to her, covering the sides of my face with kisses. I could feel her whiskers. Then she grabbed Vicki and showered her with kisses. All through the service, she kept peeking at us and sparkling, radiating sheer delight in our presence.

"She kiss now," Adriana said, loudly.

Her mother gave her a reproving look.

Adriana whispered. "She kiss now."

We prayed, we sang, we listened as the pastor preached and the a cappella choir lifted glorious voices. I didn't understand many words, but the love and joy rang out loud and clear. One after another, people stood up to share or to pray, with melodic words and expressive faces. Even the men cried openly, unashamed.

"He cry now," my young translator said.

The word I heard the most was one I already knew. *"Mulţumesc."* Thank you.

Mounds of bread, grapes, and apples were piled onto wooden paddles and passed down each row. We were sharing in the bounty of people who had so little and thanked God for providing all they needed. "We eat now," Adriana said. When the baskets were passed for an offering, I noticed that everyone threw coins in. No one was too poor to give something back to God out of hearts spilling over with gratitude.

The service lasted three hours. I knew it had ended when Adriana said, "We go now." Small children sat still the entire time. If anyone started to wiggle, a mother or grandmother would just look at the child and he would stop.

Vicki and I had already named the old lady on our bench The Kissing Lady. As we stood talking in the courtyard, she spied Bill and Dan, grabbed their necks, and covered them with kisses too.

The pastor came and introduced himself to us. He spoke perfect English. "I see you have met our beautiful lady," he said. "She is deaf, and her husband is blind."

He went on to explain that The Kissing Lady was born Jewish and barely survived the Holocaust. In the concentration camp, she learned about Jesus and gave Him her life. After the war, when religion was banned in Romania, she grew in her new faith through underground prayer groups.

He told us that believers would arrive at a certain apartment every 15 minutes, over the space of several hours. Black shades darkened the windows so no one could possibly know how many people were crammed inside. Each prayer group would have a different book, torn from one Bible. After they finished studying and memorizing it, they would pass it off in secret to another group, in exchange for their book. Not many people in Romania had ever seen a whole Bible in one piece. In fact, the pastor said that Bibles that were sent from Christians in the West were confiscated at the border and turned into toilet paper.

My brothers and sisters in that courtyard had learned how to hide God's Word in their hearts. They did not take a single precious word from that Book for granted.

The Kissing Lady and her husband outside our church.

41

Adriana (my young translator) and me at church.

The Kissing Lady gave us all one more round of sloppy kisses, and then we went home, forever changed.

During my first couple of months in Bucharest, I had been invited to several flats for dinner. Each time, the mother stayed in the kitchen all evening, cooking a feast. The daughter carted the food out, while other members of the family entertained me. No one had dining room tables. They set the coffee table with their finest lace, and I sat on the sofa to eat cabbage rolls called *sarmale* or something like grits called *mamaliga*. The family spent their entire month's ration of meat for one dinner to show hospitality to a foreigner.

One particular evening stands out. The television blared at the Nicolescus' while the preparations were underfoot. On the news, we watched a tractor being dug out of a field on one of the collective farms. A boy and his father had buried it 45 years earlier, because they didn't want the Communists to take their tractor, a fairly expensive item to own in those days. The father had died, and now the grown son unearthed the tractor. After he pulled it out, he hopped on. The tractor started.

We cheered. Domnul Nicolescu held his two hands over his heart and yelled, "Bravo!" I watched a tear escape from the corner of his eye and slowly trace a well-worn path to the tip of his chin.

There were two things I needed to experience to understand Romania, and I wasn't looking forward to either of them. I needed to visit an orphanage and a cemetery.

Heroes' Cemetery housed about 400 graves of the victims of the revolution. The tombstones were still a brilliant white, since they had existed less than a year. Every tombstone had the same date of death—December 21, 1989. Most of the birth years were between 1967 and 1971. In one corner of the cemetery, the tombstones read Mathematics Faculty. Next to them were the Aeronautics Faculty, History, Languages, Engineering. The graves all held the bodies of young college students.

Our language professors had tried to speak of being holed up inside the History Faculty, doing triage on wounded students, but their words often drowned in their tears. As young people, shot and bleeding, were carted into the classroom, these professors trained in grammar had to decide who had a chance to be saved. Nightmares of students dying in their arms haunted them.

Flowers and photographs adorned most of the graves. I copied many of the epitaphs word-for-word, looking up the ones I didn't know in my dictionary at home.

The first victim of the revolution in Bucharest, a 19-year-old named Mickey, yelled, "Down with Communism," and offered flowers to the troops. They offered him three mortal bullets in return.

Luiza said, "Liberty will not be brought to us on a platter. Do not run. They will not shoot at us. They cannot kill all of us." But one bullet stopped the enthusiasm of this revolutionary.

Bogdan, who was 21 years old, had constructed barricades and seen the blood of his friends flowing. He said, "Mama, in the life of every person a train exists. You must know when to catch it. For me this train is now. Now or never, this is the chance of my life."

The family of a fallen 18-year-old wrote, "You and so many others sacrificed for a holy and bright aim: freedom. Your heroism will remain eternally in our hearts full of gratitude. Claudiu, we will never forget you."

Răzvan, 20 years old, said, "I cannot stay at home when people die on the street for my freedom. I have to go." He died with not one bullet, but 10 bullets.

Sorin, who was only 19, said, "I will go, if there will be a need. I will sacrifice myself, so that you will have a life that is better. If I do not go, others will not go, and what will happen?" And so he went. He paid the ultimate sacrifice.

Many tombstones bore the same phrase at the end, "The assassins are not yet punished."

Heroes' Cemetery.

Romanian orphanages resembled concentration camps. The children looked like miniature inmates, heads shaven because of lice, dressed in blue and white striped pajamas. Iron bars separated them from the outside world, and often they were chained to their beds. The official reason stated they were chained for their own safety due to the lack of workers to watch out for them.

I was struck by how affectionate the children were. They were warm and gentle and would not let go. When the time came for us to leave, the children reached their hands through the iron fence to touch us until the last possible minute. Kids I knew in America would not have paid such attention to me, or minded so much when I left. They would have been busy with their toys and games. They would not have been as needy. They would not have clung so fiercely.

Soon after the revolution, foreign money started pouring in to help the plight of the orphans. Conditions were improved, more workers were hired, and they were trained to care for children with special needs. Life became a tiny bit brighter.

Most of the children in the orphanages were not orphans. Their parents were not able to take care of them because of their handicaps, either physical or mental. They were given over to the state, which provided their basic needs and nothing more. Most of the parents refused to release their children to be adopted by other families, dooming them to spend their entire lives in the custody of the state, often being moved to an asylum when they became adults.

I knew some fine Romanian couples who longed to adopt a child. The young wives were unable to bear children because they had been butchered by doctors who "cured" their menstrual problems by performing hysterectomies. If these women survived the infections and complications sure to follow, they were doomed to a childless life, while "orphans" had no families.

Occasionally, I saw American couples at the consulate, trying to adopt. The Americans received babies, because they could pay more than the Romanians. One of my Romanian friends, Cornelia, was the first to point out to me that the babies they were taking home were gypsies. "See, the baby's skin is darker than Romanians," she said.

The demand for orphans had created an ugly supply. Cornelia said that young gypsy girls were raped by the men in their community, who sold their babies for thousands of dollars to rich Americans desperate for children. These good-hearted Westerners thought they were rescuing the homeless children they had seen on the television news, but those children remained locked in the orphanages.

Male leaders controlled the entire gypsy tribe. At birth, certain babies were chosen and given the honor of becoming the beggar for the community. The baby's legs were purposely crippled. Sometimes the feet were broken so the bones would fuse together with the feet facing backward. As these children grew, they were set down on the streets, where they would cry for money all day long.

People would drop coins into their tin cups, moved by compassion for the plight of these poor, crippled children and feeble old women, the other beggars for the tribe. The panhandlers were dressed in tattered rags, without shoes or socks or coats, no matter how cold outside. They never saw the money. The men of the tribe drank the donations.

As winter approached, several of the women in my church got busy knitting child-size socks, gloves, hats, and scarves. Cornelia invited me to go downtown with a group she organized one day. We walked to the largest metro stations, where most of the beggars sat. We personally put the socks and gloves on the children, hoping that the men would leave them. We touched the children, smiled at them, and told them that Jesus loves them.

It wasn't much, but it was something.

I observed how bureaucracy reigned in post-Communist countries when we registered to be students at the University of Bucharest. Form after form had to be signed, stamped profusely, and sealed. Every office had a Romanian man in charge of the works, barking orders to the women secretaries who scurried around like frightened mice. Dressed in worn suits and tall fleecy hats, the bosses commanded respect. We had to call them Domnul (or Mr.) Chief Popescu or Dumitrescu or whatever "escu" they were.

Finally, we made it to the last stop. This boss noticed me in the long line and waved me to the front, commenting on my smile. It made me rather embarrassed, yet my team and I liked the special treatment. Bill and Dan teased me that I smiled on purpose, hoping to get us all bumped up. If I did, it was subconscious.

We sat silently inside the office of the Chief of All Chiefs at the University, as he shuffled our papers and studied them.

"Miss Richardson, there is a big problem. A mistake on your *pașaport.*"

Bill, Dan, and Vicki were all about 10 years younger than I, and the chief was convinced we were the same age. He informed me that my birth year had been written incorrectly, and it should be 1966, not 1956. I tried to tell him that 1956 was right, but he refused to listen. He took it upon himself to set the record straight. He issued my student *legitimație* card (making me legitimate) with my revised birth year, changing my age from 33 to 23. I felt like kissing him.

Just for fun, when we got our new passport photos taken, the four of us jumped in one picture together. Bill tried to get 10 extra copies made of our group photo. He picked up the envelope of pictures and discovered that the man had cropped out the other three and printed 30 copies of just me.

For my early November birthday, the guys handed out these photos of me to our teachers, several students, the bread man, people at the *piaţa*, the chief, everyone I saw on a daily basis. The guys asked them to help me celebrate.

Our team passport photo (L–R: Dan, me, Vicki, Bill).

My birthday with the team: photos of me cropped from the group passport picture became party favors.

The morning of my birthday, as I walked to language class and went about my routine, people would step out of their shops and surprise me by saying, *"La mulți ani!"* or, "to many more years." Besides birthdays, this all-purpose greeting worked for New Year's, Christmas, or whenever anyone sneezed.

It was one of the most fun birthdays of my life. At my party that night, Dan said, "This whole country is in love with you, Taryn."

That seemed significant to me, because I had spent the last two years of my life imagining a relationship with a guy who clearly was not in love with me. Max's flirtatiousness led me and my friends to assume he cared. His words said that we were just friends, but his actions disputed that.

Whenever Max hinted about having feelings for me, the very next day he ignored me completely. Our relationship shifted off and on this way for months. I gave him control over my emotions. I felt happy when he seemed to be interested in me, and depressed when he didn't. I looked to him to know how to feel each day, being yanked up and down as though I was a yo-yo. Max held the string.

I tried so hard to be what he wanted me to be, but I just kept messing up. I kept falling back to being myself. Sometimes I laughed loudly in public, and he would roll his eyes. Or I ate more than carrot sticks, and he'd whisper that I really didn't need that. I remember mispronouncing a French word, and he corrected me with an exasperated voice.

I hadn't realized how much I needed to put time and space between Max and myself. In Romania, I felt as though I had been set free. I could be myself, and I could enjoy life.

Romanians liked it when I laughed loudly, because it showed my zest for life. Strangers told me I was pretty; they didn't tell me to eat less. People praised me for speaking Romanian. I knew my pronunciation needed a lot of work, but they claimed I had a charming accent.

The people I now lived among accepted me just the way I was. That brought tremendous freedom to my soul. I went to Romania to teach them true freedom in Christ, but I received just as much as I gave. I don't know why Romanians seemed to be drawn to me. Perhaps they liked the artist's soul that we shared. I only know I did nothing to deserve or earn it. God in His goodness let me see a glimpse of His grace mirrored in the Romanians. And it helped my heart heal from Max.

The most ordinary people showered me with unexpected kindnesses—the peasant woman who gave me free flowers, the chief who changed my birth year to make me 10 years younger, the old lady in my church who plastered me with kisses. I felt overwhelmed by God's grace in Romania, a land that had seemed destitute at first glance. Looking deeper, I discovered the true beauty of Romania—its people.

I wondered if God had it in mind all along for me to live in Romania. It no longer felt like a fluke assignment. I had come home at last.

God supplied just what I needed, answering my prayer from the heap in Vienna. He lavished me with enough grace to live in a place with plenty of rats but very little water. Now it was my turn to spread that grace around.

What About You?

- Think of the Kissing Ladies in your life—people who exhibit quiet strength and deep faith in difficult circumstances. What have you learned from them?

- Can you think of people who have demonstrated God's grace to you by unexpected kindnesses? How did you feel?

- How can you pass this same grace on to others?

Chapter 4

HAPPY HOLY DAYS

Jesus said, "Truly I say to you, there is no one who has left house
or brothers or sisters or mother or father or children or farms,
for My sake and for the gospel's sake, but that he shall receive
a hundred times as much now in the present age, houses and
brothers and sisters and mothers and children and farms,
along with persecutions; and in the age to come,
eternal life."

—Mark 10:29–30

November 1990, Bucharest, Romania

I BRACED MYSELF to feel especially homesick as the
Thanksgiving and Christmas season approached. As a team,
we couldn't be passive about holidays. We had to intentionally
plan how to integrate our American traditions into the season
and make it fun. We would build new memories. After all, we
were family now.

The days had grown colder, and the grayness outside
matched my mood. The government hadn't turned on the heat

yet, and we needed it. I missed my family and friends. I missed America.

We had only received mail once in the two months we had been there, and we had no telephones. E-mail and cell phones didn't exist in 1990. Because of security reasons, I gave my friends an address in Germany. Whenever one of our supervisors would make a trip to check on us, they would bring our mail. Max had not written. The letters I did receive were worn thin from reading them so often.

Our team, the five long-term members and the four of us Stinters, made plans to celebrate Thanksgiving. The wives on the long-term team had come prepared for all the year's holidays. Wendy and Marian brought decorations for Christmas, Easter, Valentine's Day, Fourth of July, even birthdays. Wendy arrived in Romania with cans of pumpkin, corn, and peas tucked into her suitcase, earmarked for Thanksgiving.

Marian bought already-kneaded dough from the *pâine* store to make dinner rolls and pumpkin pie crust. Vicki and I were in charge of mashed potatoes. The selection at the *piaţa* had grown scarce, but we did buy some wrinkled potatoes with long eyes.

None of us could find the one remaining dish anywhere. We still needed the most important part of the Thanksgiving meal—the turkey. When I made "gobble, gobble" noises in the *piaţa*, I learned the word for turkey is *curcan*. Everyone we asked agreed there were no *curcans* in Bucharest. Eastern European meals usually involved cabbage, and if fortunate enough to have meat, it would be pork.

We contemplated substituting a chicken. After all, both are poultry. But the chickens were so scrawny that we joked they were killed by starvation. Only a turkey would do for our Thanksgiving feast.

Bill, Dan, Vicki, and I prayed every day for a couple of weeks before Thanksgiving. "Father, we know this isn't anything important, but we also know that You love us, and You love to give us good gifts. You tell us in Your Word to ask, so that's what we're doing. We are asking You to please provide a turkey. It would mean an awful lot to us, but whether You say yes or no, we will still love You, and we will still believe that You love us." We waited for His answer.

In the evenings, international students from Arab countries made their way door-to-door through the Foreign Student Dorms. They peddled warm-up suits or demitasse cups. Every time they came, they had entirely different stock. We referred to it as the Home Shopping Hour.

The night before Thanksgiving, we heard a knock at our door. Vicki jumped up to answer, expectant. Two young Arab men stood there with a bulging duffle bag.

Our common language was Romanian, a new language for all of us. I asked what they had to sell.

One of them answered. The word didn't sound like curcan, but I couldn't understand what he said with his thick accent. It didn't matter, because I knew what they had brought to sell us. I knew God's character and had experienced these kinds of coincidences so many times before that I had grown to anticipate them.

The other guy reached into the duffel bag, and my heart did a flutter kick. He pulled out…. a soccer ball.

"Is that all?" I asked, stunned.

Yes, that was all they had.

I pushed back hot tears. My hopes had screeched to a halt.

I made my way to the bathroom to cry alone. "Lord, was this too much to ask? We've given up so much to be here. Do we have to give up a turkey, too?"

The next day, the group began to assemble in Mark and Wendy's room for our Thanksgiving meal. Besides the nine Americans on the team, we had invited several Romanian students, all newly serious about following Christ. One of our supervisors had just arrived unexpectedly from Germany, carrying a bag full of our mail that was difficult to ignore. *I wish he had put a turkey in that bag.*

A vase of mums stood in the center of Wendy's serving table. One by one, we added our offerings, in chipped enamel pans. No one had pretty serving dishes. I didn't mind.

We waited for Daniel and Marian, the last to arrive. Suddenly there arose a clatter at the door. Daniel entered with a pan spilling over with a plumpish turkey. Even Santa with a sack would not have been a more welcome sight.

We bombarded Daniel with questions. He had bartered for a turkey the night before with one of his many connections. He and Marian had decided to surprise us. They succeeded.

Our turkey did not come the way I had expected. It didn't matter. We had a turkey. My immediate response of discouragement the night before didn't stop God from giving.

Our first Thanksgiving (L–R: Vicki, John, me).

As we gathered around, John, the single guy on the long-term team, explained to the Romanians about the original Thanksgiving. He said the Pilgrims wanted to thank God for bringing them through the first winter in their new land, and to share their bounty with their new friends. We did too. He went on to say that the Bible tells us to remember what God has done for us in the past and to thank Him for His blessings. John gave us an opportunity to remember aloud.

"I'm grateful for this turkey," Dan said. "It shows that God cares about the smallest details that touch our lives."

The Romanians chimed in.

"I have new life in Christ."

"I thank God for sending you to us to tell us about Jesus."

"Finally we have freedom, and it is a precious thing."

Their joy reminded me, once again, of my purpose in being there, worth every sacrifice in my spartan lifestyle.

"When I left the States, I told everyone I care about how much they mean to me, and they said the same things back," I said. "I will always treasure those words—words that may have remained unspoken if I hadn't come here to Romania. I don't take friendships for granted now."

We grasped each other's hands and thanked God together for His goodness to us.

The small dorm room overflowed with hard-backed chairs scattered about. Many of us sat cross-legged on the double bed as we ate from mismatched plates and tin-tasting flatware.

I realized that I had never experienced a better Thanksgiving. Our turkey, a gift from God's hands, tasted divine. Never before had I felt more grateful during any of the holidays I had celebrated in the States.

After the meal, we walked downtown to get tickets for the latest American movie, still a novelty in Bucharest. *Karate Kid Part II* was playing, several years after its opening in the States. The seats had sold out hours ago, but standing is always an option in a country without fire marshal codes. We stood in the back for two hours, alongside our Romanian friends, watching the entire movie on our feet.

In America, usually after the big meal, I would waddle to the couch, stuffed, and fall asleep in front of a football game or *Miracle on 34th Street*. I had never stood up during an entire movie in my life, certainly never on Thanksgiving night.

We could handle anything that day, because God had given us our turkey. Besides, we knew that our bag of letters sat waiting for us when we got back to the dorm. Vicki and I stayed up until the middle of the night, devouring every word, laughing and crying as we recounted some of our news to each other.

I had expected this to be a crummy holiday. Instead we created new memories. I had a feeling that the simplicity and deep significance of this Thanksgiving could set the standard for all Thanksgivings to come.

The days turned slowly after Thanksgiving. It seemed as though Christmas would never arrive. A few events, some small and some significant, helped the time pass.

One weekend, the whole team took a short train ride to a charming village in the mountains for some much needed rest. Vicki and I wanted to check out the neighboring town of Braşov. Everyone else decided to stay put, so we left by ourselves. We boarded a train north for a 20-minute ride, having tickets to return to Predeal two hours later, at 2:00. We toured the Black Church, a Gothic Lutheran cathedral that got its name after surviving a fire in 1689, and then sauntered through the quaint, old town square before heading back to board our train.

When our return train didn't stop after 20 minutes, we started to notice that the scenery wasn't familiar. Beginning to get nervous, I asked the people in our compartment when we would arrive in Predeal.

"No, we go to Sighişoara," several said. "We go north. Predeal is south."

The realization of what had happened sunk like a stone to the pit of my stomach.

"How long to Sighişoara?"

"Two hours."

Vicki and I knew our teammates would worry about us, but there was nothing we could do. We jumped off the train in Sighişoara, and were able to board another one, going in the right direction this time, within 30 minutes. That meant that we would arrive at 7:00 in the evening, five hours late. We didn't bother to hunt for a telephone in Sighişoara, since there were none in our hostel back in Predeal.

We relinquished our passports to the conductor, necessary for any foreign traveler at that time, even though we were not crossing a border. As we got closer to Predeal, though, we became anxious that we would not get them back in time. When the conductor returned to our cabin, I asked him for our passports.

"Come with me," he said.

I left Vicki alone and followed the conductor through five cars, none of them lit. I counted carefully so I could find Vicki again. The conductor stopped at a door with thick chains across it. I took a step back. He unlocked the chains and grabbed at me, trying to pull me into the compartment with him.

I screamed. "No. *Nu e bine.* It is not good."

He lunged, jabbing me in the crotch.

I ran until I reached the end of the car. Then I turned to yell, "*American paşaport. Imediat.*"

I knew I needed to make a commotion, to draw attention to his actions. Several heads popped out of cabins as I shouted. I had my witnesses. I counted on the fact that Romanians had a healthy fear of offending American citizens. It worked. The conductor threw our two passports at me, onto the floor of the

57

car. I scooped them up and staggered, stunned, back five cars to Vicki. I walked past her in the dark.

Vicki opened the door. "Taryn, here I am. Are you OK?"

I told her something awful had happened, but I couldn't talk about it. I felt so foolish. I should have known better than to follow him in the dark. There are more important things than passports. Vicki put her arms around me, and we sat in silence for the next few minutes.

When we arrived in Predeal, Bill stood on the platform. He had not moved for five hours. "My girls, my girls!" he cried. We ran to his outstretched arms, burrowing our faces in his fluffy down jacket.

We continued speaking in classrooms, and had more students to talk with about Jesus than we could handle. Among us, we knew of 30 students who had begun to follow Jesus in the three months we'd lived there. We gathered the new believers into Bible study groups in dorm rooms, going from one group to another, until we could no longer stay awake.

When we showed the *Jesus* film in the dorms, students would hang on every word and openly sob as they watched Jesus being crucified. They were unashamed of others seeing their response and their raw emotion.

In the States, I'd ministered in some tough places—Berkeley and New England. I enjoyed strategizing the most effective ways to communicate God's timeless message so it would be heard and understood. Here, people were so ravenous to know about Christ that we didn't have time to strategize. We depended solely on the Holy Spirit, not on our smart plans. We made sure our hearts were right before God, built relationships, told them flat out about Jesus, and trusted God with the results. With such a ripe harvest, we merely picked the fruit off the trees. I'd never seen anything like it before. I felt exhilarated.

Every evening we stumbled home, too tired to trek up the crooked stairs. I would climb into the shadowy elevator, which rarely stopped flush with the floor. In the dark void, I didn't know if anyone else was aboard or how to brace myself for the landing, whether my descent would be merely a large step down or a jump of four feet. One time I thought I was alone in the lift until I felt a breath on my neck. I screamed.

We met as a team every week to pray together and touch base with how things were going. Dan, with his strong Midwestern work ethic, usually said we needed to work harder, that we weren't doing enough. I often expressed our need to focus on being and not just doing, to take time for ourselves so our ministry would be out of an overflow and not scraping the dregs of the barrel. Vicki just smiled her mischievous smile and stayed out of it.

Bill wanted everyone to be happy and didn't like negative comments. He felt the burden as our leader when things were not quite right.

Every morning as we walked to language school, Bill would ask in his most polite Southern way, "Did you sleep well?" He meant it like "how are you"—a question not intended to be answered honestly.

I usually said "no," and then proceeded to complain about the noise or my headache or how something on my mind kept me awake. I knew he wanted me to smile sweetly and say, "I slept great," but I had to be authentic. Bill didn't want reality.

He struggled with language, and a realistic person could have predicted that he'd never make it in Romania. Bill proved that communication can transcend words. People saw his heart and flocked to him. Children followed him everywhere, grabbing at his pockets for treats. Sometimes he doled out child-sized toothbrushes (his father, the dentist, kept him well-supplied) and Snickers bars. After the candy, Bill demonstrated the fine art of dental hygiene while the kids brushed and giggled.

Bill and Dan came home one day to see a rat eating crumbs on their kitchen table. Somehow the rodent had climbed up there. Now we knew for sure how the flower tops had been broken off and carted into the bathroom. The guys had a new mission: to hunt down and capture rats. They worked every free moment on designing traps, finally settling on one involving Tupperware with peanut butter as the bait. By Christmas, they had caught six rats in their room and three in ours. Each time a rat wandered into the trap, the guys would sprint to get Daniel, Mark, and John. While the boys whooped it up on the balcony, taking turns hurtling the rat to certain death, Vicki and I would cringe from a safe distance. I realized how little I understood men.

One night I dreamed that Max and I were driving on the beach in a jeep. He yanked the steering wheel and headed straight into the water. As the ocean poured into our jeep, I raised myself up in the seat, yelled *"Niciodata!"* and swam to shore, leaving Max behind. I woke up, heart pounding, unsure of what *niciodata* meant.

My dictionary said it meant "nevermore." Scores of Romanian words were trapped in my subconscious mind, words I had heard once or twice but couldn't recall upon demand. I had read that our brains continue to process language information, sorting it into categories, while we sleep. Somehow, I had heard that word before, and my mind conjured it up in my dream. My brain tried to tell me that Max was poison to me. He didn't care whether or not he hurt me. Even in my sleep, I knew I needed to tell him "nevermore."

This Christmas would be the first in 45 years that Romanian factories would be closed. No one I knew had ever had a day off work for Christmas. There were no Christmas decorations. Students searched for hours for gifts for their families. Many bought a precious bar of soap for their mothers. I thought of the holiday being taken for granted or filled with meaningless excess in my own country. Here in Bucharest, the excitement to celebrate Christmas was palpable, even without decorations and with only meager gifts.

Often when I returned home to my door, I would find notes written by Romanian friends who had come to visit. "Happy Holy Days" was the common greeting this time of year. I realized that holiday is a shortened version of holy day.

Underneath one "Happy Holy Day" note, I read the words, "If you are boring, come talk to me." It was signed by a guy named Liviu. *I wonder why he likes boring girls. Maybe Liviu just has a high threshold for boredom, as my seminary professor liked to describe doctoral students.* I learned a valuable language lesson: the letters at the end of words like "excited" and "exciting" can make a big difference in meaning.

Early in December, we started to coax our undercover ministry out in the open. The *Jesus* film premiered at a cinema in downtown Bucharest, the last capital city in Eastern Europe to host the debut. People lined up for blocks to get inside, standing in the sub-freezing temperatures, dressed in their nicest outfits. The premiere had all the decorum of a typical Communist event. Several leaders of Campus Crusade, some from our headquarters in Eastern Europe and some from the States, came for this historic event. Not understanding the thrill of movies for people who had been deprived this pleasure, several thought the long lines indicated peoples' interest in hearing about Jesus. Romanians did want to know about Jesus, but the line for the thriller *Black Widow*, just the week before, had been almost as long.

The days turned bitterly cold, yet we didn't have even one drop of heat, and often no electricity. Sometimes I had to wash my hair by candlelight, with no way to dry it. We all had colds, and mine lingered until I saw white spots in the back of my throat. Dan doled out penicillin to me from his stash of antibiotics. I only got worse. I couldn't wait to get to the West and a doctor.

Nothing struck fear in the heart of a Romanian more than dentists and doctors. Most adults had rotten and missing teeth, unwilling to see a dentist because they didn't administer Novocain. Like characters straight out of Charles Dickens, they tied rags around their heads when the pain became unbearable. Many college students had lost parents to staph infections following routine operations. When Iulian had surgery on his compound knee fracture, without anesthesia, we Americans tried to gather up all the pain medication we could find. As I approached his hospital to smuggle in Tylenol with codeine, I saw dazed patients lumbering outside in cotton gowns, open in the back, wearing rubber boots and fleecy hats. Inside, the equipment was antiquated. Iulian put his hands on the rusty bar overhead to raise himself to a sitting position. I watched orange flakes fall down on his leg, inches from his wound.

No thanks. I would wait to see a doctor in Switzerland. I just wished I could take all my Romanian friends with me.

For a couple weeks, students lined up outside the dorms each evening to rally the cause. They planned a second revolution, one year after the first, on December 22. The National Salvation Front and Fascist parties had both been squelched by hard-line Communists in November. The students planned to march from the dorms to President Iliescu's house. It was good that we would leave for our Christmas retreat on December 20. After my classroom lectures on democracy, the students saw me as something of a catalyst and asked me to join them. I didn't want to get caught up in a political demonstration. That's not why I came to Romania.

Finally, the day arrived for us to leave for Christmas break. It had been snowing all night. We four hauled our suitcases to the lobby of our dorm, then trudged into knee-high snow to load them in Mihai's car. We had the roads to ourselves at 5:00 in the morning, which helped me relax a bit as we plowed through the drifts, headed for Otopeni Aeroport.

Once inside, we learned that all flights were delayed, obviously due to the weather. Mihai waited with us. We went to the cantina and ordered *ceai*. As always, the tea was lukewarm and served in giant cups, but the Turkish coffee in demitasse cups tasted hot and quite strong.

The airport had no heat. Guards stood 10 feet apart on the parapets, their fingers resting on the triggers of rifles pointed down at the crowd. Many windows were broken, and the ceiling had huge gaps. Pigeons flew around at the top of the ceiling. A few of them pooped on Bill's head as we drank our tea. We joked that Bill had a bull's eye painted on top of his knit cap.

We all laughed, even Bill, each time another pigeon struck. We were almost giddy with excitement about our Christmas in Switzerland. We would celebrate Jesus' birth with our friends from the other Stint teams in Eastern Europe. Not even pigeon poop could dampen our spirits.

Mihai kept checking the flight status for us, and found out later that afternoon that the entire airport had closed due to a general strike. No one knew if it would reopen the next day, but we could do nothing until then.

Mihai drove us downtown, and we split apart with our different tasks, each trying to find a way out of the country. Bill and Vicki went to check train schedules, Dan went to Swiss Air and Austrian Air, and I tried to call the others at the retreat in Switzerland.

Daniel and Marian had a phone, the only one on our team. When they got it after more than a year on the waiting list, Daniel said he'd be happy if it even worked half the time. So far, he wasn't very happy. He was under-whelmed.

When they left for Germany three days earlier, they had given us a key to their room in case of emergency. I sat at Daniel and

Marian's table for six hours, dialing the number again and again. My neck ached from cradling the phone with my shoulder as my body tensed from the cold. My Christmas cheer had dissipated to desperation by now.

I sobbed and prayed as I dialed. "Father, please, please help us. I need to see a doctor about my throat, we all need to get out of this country, we need to call our parents over Christmas, we need to get our mail and be with our friends. I just can't handle it if we can't get out of Romania. I can't spend Christmas here. Oh, please. I can't take any more. Help me, Lord!"

During my ordeal of dialing, God gently reminded me that I didn't need any of those things; I merely wanted them. He whispered to my heart that He is all I need, and that He will continue to provide for me and take care of me, as He always has. "You're right. I will trust You, Lord. Help me to trust You."

At midnight, I finally reached an operator, who put me through to our retreat hostel in the Swiss Alps. I could only speak a few German words.

"*Guten Abend! Bitte schön*. Please, I must *sprechen* with American group. *Ist* important," I said.

The woman on the phone hurried to grab the closest American. Thankfully, college-age people stay up late. I explained our plight and asked if they, as a group, would pray that we could get out of the country.

The next day dawned the same. It seemed that we were all having an identical nightmare.

Mihai shuttled us early to the airport. We waited all day. To pass the time, we made up goofy songs and Top Ten Lists of Things To Do in Bucharest over Christmas, hoping to perform them for our friends. We laughed a lot, and that helped to ease the tension.

At 7:30 that evening, after a 12-hour wait, people started running for the gate. "Hurry!" Mihai yelled. "Swiss Air is open."

We joined the swelling mob. Three special planes were brought in. Swiss Air agreed to accept tickets from Tarom, the Romanian airlines, at the lower Romanian prices. We were the last four people on the last of the three planes.

As we walked through the checkpoint, we had to show our tickets, passport, and the exit papers we were given when we arrived in-country on the train. Our names were then written by hand in a ledger. Vicki didn't have her exit paper. When the official barked at her that she couldn't leave, she started to cry. So did I. We were so close to leaving. After all this, how could a tiny piece of paper hold us back?

The chivalrous official couldn't handle two young women in tears, so he waved us through. "Happy Holy Day," he said. We were free!

We walked through the unlit transit lounge, onto the tarmac, and boarded the plane, lit up like a beacon on the dark runway. We sank into plush seats, with room to stretch out. The flight attendants handed out slippers, blankets, and eye masks. We devoured the airline food. I leaned back in my seat and closed my eyes. A tear trickled down my cheek as I silently thanked God for His provision.

We arrived too late to take the train on to Wengen for our retreat. Instead we boarded a bus for downtown Zurich and found a hotel. I felt nauseous as we walked along the ancient streets, tastefully decked in white Christmas lights. Like a mole, I had been confined to darkness for months, and even this subdued light made me dizzy. We called the others at the retreat and were settled in our rooms by midnight.

December 1990, Switzerland

The next day, December 22, was the first anniversary of the revolution in Romania. We woke early to catch our train to Interlaken, then another to Lauterbrünnen, and lastly a cog train straight up the Alps to Wengen. I reveled in the pure, crisp air.

Quaint houses and shops filled our village. Rosy-cheeked women carried baskets of baked goods, and men in boiled wool jackets and feathered hats pulled children on sleds down the snowy street. There were no vehicles in Wengen. The magnificent mountains served as the backdrop for this idyllic scene.

We easily found the Edelweiss Inn. Some of our group spilled out to welcome us.

That evening, after a delicious meal of *boeuf fondu bourguignonne*, the whole group met together. The Stint teams from Poland, Czechoslovakia, Yugoslavia, and Hungary told amazing stories of how they had seen God at work. Our team joined in. Larry, the Director of Campus Crusade in Eastern Europe, challenged all of us to come back after our year ended.

"The doors are wide open right now," Larry said. "But only God knows how long they will remain open. Negative influences from the West will also come through those doors—things like pornography, cults, indifference to God. The next two years will be the most critical time to be here, the time of greatest receptivity to the gospel. We need you in Eastern Europe. We need you to stay and make disciples of all these new converts."

During the last three months, God had been stirring my heart. I realized I loved Romania, despite the fears I had in the beginning. I felt alive and needed. Yes, life was difficult, but the joy of lost people giving their lives to Christ far outweighed the hardships. I had left home and received so much more in return.

That night, I talked to Larry and told him I wanted to come back. I would add a long-term assignment (usually seven years) to my one-year stint. I knew I needed to write to my parents first, to make sure they wouldn't worry about me. But I felt certain that God was calling me to make Romania my permanent home.

After I made my decision official, I found a bag of mail sitting outside my door. As I devoured the letters, I saw my first one from Max. I hadn't thought of him all evening. I made the decision apart from him, without being swayed by his on-again, off-again feelings for me. His letter arrived too late. He was irrelevant to my plans. I had moved on.

The next four days were filled with friends, skating, shopping, skiing, and talking late at night over steaming cups of cocoa in front of blazing fires. We prayed together with tears and laughter. I visited a clinic where the doctor told me I had a drug fever from taking antibiotics for too long. He told me to stop taking them, and I started to feel better right away. I got in line at the phone booth outside to call my parents, my brother, and my best friend. It was the first time I had talked to them in three months.

On Christmas Eve, many of us walked down the hill to attend a beautiful Anglican service of praise. Back at the hostel, we had our gift exchange, each choosing a present that someone on another team had brought. I received a tape of beautiful a cappella Romanian Christmas carols by the Madrigal choir, from the team in Prague. Nothing like this was available in Romania.

Bill had a skiing accident that day while he, a mere novice, attempted to teach Dan and Vicki how to ski. He got turned around and started sliding backward down the mountain, crying "Whoa, whoa, whoa!" When he tried to stop, the tip of his ski flew up and jammed the top of his nose. Skin flapped down over his eyes. Doctors stitched up the bloody mess, making one long line of eyebrow. Since medical conditions were not sanitary in Romania, the decision was made for our whole team to stay in Germany until Bill's stitches would be removed. We had arrived three days late, but now we would have seven extra days.

We awoke on Christmas morning to delicious aromas wafting from our Swiss kitchen. We gathered around the tree and opened the gifts our families had sent months before to our headquarters in Germany. That afternoon, we joined the villagers, trudging up the mountain to encircle the tallest fir tree, holding white candles, and singing *Stille Nacht,* while a light snow quietly dusted us, enveloping us in peaceful contentedness. It was a holy moment.

The day after Christmas, we all left the Edelweiss and headed to Zurich. The others returned to their assignments, but my team hopped on a train for Basel, Switzerland. There we were met by one of the headquarter's staff, who drove us across the German border to a Black Forest hamlet called Kandern. Here we snuggled into our director's empty house, slept late each morning, wrote letters, read, hiked in the snow, and even shopped for the groceries we would need to last until June. My brother had sent my favorite Christmas video, *It's a Wonderful Life*, along with footage of my toddler and baby nephews. As a team, we shared everything, whether videos or family. My teammates were almost as eager as I to watch the antics of Alex and Mark.

I wrote to my parents, explaining why I was sure God wanted me to stay in Romania long-term. I told them that I needed to know what they thought. I couldn't go if my decision was going to make life unbearable for my parents. I asked them to each respond individually. Finally, as an independent woman of 34, I was learning to honor my parents and respect their wisdom.

When the time came to return to Romania, I felt rested and refreshed. I had started the holy day season feeling homesick. I ended it with the comforting realization that I had found my home.

What About You?

- Have you ever been surprised to find that you feel at home somewhere you never thought you would? How do you recognize home?

- You don't have to be stuck in an airport in Romania at Christmas to feel desperate for something. How do you handle that?

- Think of times you have seen God's provision in an unexpected way, like the turkey for Thanksgiving. What would your response be if God never provided what you asked for?

- How do you decide about something it seems God may be calling you to do?

Chapter 5

THE HEART OF ROMANIA

*The Lord will keep you from all harm—he will watch
over your life; the Lord will watch over your coming
and going both now and forevermore.*

—Psalm 121:7–8 (NIV)

February 1991, Prague, Czechoslovakia

AS I ENTERED the girls' apartment in Prague, I saw Vicki. She wasn't supposed to be there. She should have returned to Romania by now. We had flown together to Prague, where Vicki stayed with the Stint team, who were her age, while I went on to spend a week with women my age.

It was only our second trip out of the country.

"Vicki, what are you doing here?"

"Well…when I got to the airport, they said my flight had already left."

"What time did you get there?"

"I don't know. Sometime in the afternoon—"

"But it was a morning flight."

"Well, I know that now." Vicki rolled her eyes.

"Don't you remember, before I left, I told you that your flight was in the morning?" I felt like an interrogator. I needed a bare light bulb.

"I was wondering why you kept saying that, and then I got to the airport—"

"Did you call the team so they wouldn't worry?"

"No, I couldn't find their number."

I sighed. "Well, at least you were able to get our groceries." I saw her raise her eyebrows. "You did get the groceries, didn't you?"

"Well…I kinda lost the grocery list. I think it was with the phone number. Hey, I'm sorry, Taryn. I didn't do it on purpose. I knew when you got here, you'd have the phone number and the grocery list."

I sighed again. I'd just returned from such a rejuvenating time, and already, I felt frustrated. All the good effects of the week, and poof, they disappeared in an instant. Why did I have to take care of all the details for myself and for her? She was an adult, too, and I wasn't her mother.

I had traveled with Melanie from Prague to a tiny Austrian village nestled in the Tyrolean Alps. We had been invited to a ski retreat with the single staff women from all over Eastern Europe, part of the long-term teams in their respective countries. Melanie and I were also Campus Crusade staff members, but we led Stint teams made up of students just out of college, like Vicki.

My goal for the week had been fellowship, and I received that, and so much more. My faith was stretched in the presence of those courageous women, many of whom had lived alone behind the Iron Curtain for years. I was in awe of them.

Kasia, who took on a Polish name for security and then kept it, told stories of life under martial law. Tears flowed as women recounted a friend's rape and return to the States to heal. Another teammate, a young mother, had died suddenly, leaving questions of whether she would have been resuscitated if she lived in the

States. Dear Gwen had been notified in-country that her father, and then her brother, had died. She had not been able to say good-bye to them.

These faithful women had counted the cost and paid dearly. I felt privileged to be in their presence and hoped I could live up to their example.

Abruptly, I had to re-enter my life. My life with no older woman to mentor me. Instead I had a younger woman who depended on me. I hadn't signed up for this.

My tour of Prague now had to include stops at the airline office to change Vicki's ticket, the telegram office to notify the team in Romania, and the grocery store. Since Czechoslovakia operated much more efficiently than Romania, we accomplished more than one errand in the same day, with time left over to see the main sights.

The fairy tale city, with over a thousand years of history, enthralled me with its medieval spires and winding alleyways. We arrived at Old Town Hall in time to see the hourly dance of the apostles along the face of its astronomical clock. In the center of the square sat the massive bronze statue of Jan Hus, martyred in 1415 for spreading the gospel. Melanie and I took a break at a café once frequented by Franz Kafka and other dissidents, overlooking the Vltava River. The Charles Bridge pulsed with artists selling their etchings, while the soulful music of saxophones and violins wafted overhead. I counted 30 Baroque statues of saints along the old stone bridge. We stood at the spot in Wenceslas Square where the student Jan Palach sacrificed his life in 1968 for freedom, during Prague Spring. We wandered through the Jewish Quarter, past the cemetery with 20,000 graves stacked 12 layers deep, where an unanswered question haunted me. *How could a city this beautiful have been so deadly to so many?*

The next afternoon, the Czechoslovakian team deposited Vicki and me at the airport, and we settled in for our flight home on Tarom, Romania's airline. Like all airports in the former Communist bloc, officers with machine guns patrolled.

We boarded our small propeller plane and took off for our short flight to Bucharest. Vicki and I read our books and gave each other space. I didn't feel like chatting with her, still bothered from the day before. I know I communicated that quite well, non-verbally of course.

Tarom was making progress. This plane had a no-smoking section, a novelty in Eastern Europe. The passengers seated on the right side were allowed to smoke, but the passengers on the left could not. I figured the concept still needed tweaking.

At 7:00 that evening, the time we were supposed to land, the lights on the runway below appeared as diamonds on black velvet. Our Tarom plane hovered over the Otopeni Aeroport. Suddenly the lights went out on the runway. We continued circling. Finally, the pilot spoke on the intercom.

"We are not landing in Bucharest." That was all he told us.

I overheard a flight attendant explain to other passengers that we couldn't land because of the fog. I wondered how I could see the runway lights through such dense fog.

An hour later, our plane touched down. Somewhere. We had no idea where, not even which country.

I could get by with my basic Romanian by this time, but most of the passengers didn't speak Romanian at all. Finally, one of the flight attendants came out of the cockpit.

"Where are we?" I asked.

"Sibiu, the heart of Romania. It's in the center of the country."

We continued to sit on the plane. We waited in the cold darkness. I felt anxious.

Vicki and I broke our silence and whispered to each other, trying to make sense of what was happening. We prayed quietly that God would keep us safe.

I studied the other people on board. Besides the crew, I counted 10 passengers. There were two couples speaking Slavic languages (I wasn't sure which ones), three German businessmen, an Asian man, and us—the two Americans.

After about an hour, the outside door opened. A voice called for the Polish ambassador to follow him. A couple got up and left the plane.

The rest of us continued to sit. I started to feel that familiar pain. *No, it couldn't be. Not now. Not here.* I wasn't supposed to start my period for a couple more days.

Another hour passed. The door opened and a male voice gruffly said, "*Hai!* Come on, hurry up!"

We grabbed our carry-on bags, felt our way down the stairs, and followed this disembodied voice along the inky tarmac. I sat closest to the door, so I climbed out of the plane first.

Our escort whispered to me, "Hey, I am Communist pig. Be careful for me. Would you like to hear joke?"

"OK." I didn't know how to respond.

"Do you know why it was not scientist who invented Communism?"

I hesitated. "No, I don't know."

"A scientist would have tested it on dogs first. A scientist would not have tested it on people before dogs."

I didn't know whether he would be angry if I didn't laugh at his joke, or if he'd shoot me on the spot if I did. So I politely murmured, "Mmmmm."

We were marched single file into the terminal and told to sit in the waiting room. A Tarom official announced that once Customs people came to check our passports, we would be taken to a hotel in Sibiu to spend the night.

Since we were international passengers in a domestic airport, they couldn't just let us out to wander around Romania. Sibiu didn't have x-ray scanners. For that matter, the main airport in the capital city didn't have scanners, computers, or even conveyor belts for luggage.

I asked the "Communist pig" who had escorted us if there was a telephone I could use. "I need to call my friends in Bucharest. They will be worried."

He called to another guard to watch our group while he led me to the telephone. We went upstairs to a door marked *Securitate Telecomunicație,* with a picture of a skull and crossbones over the words *Strict Interzis,* or strictly forbidden. Inside were several huge machines with reel-to-reel tapes and headphones. I stood in one of the Secret Police listening rooms. I forgot to be frightened, excited by the adventure. Not many other Americans had ever seen the inside of one of these rooms, the existence of which was constantly denied officially.

I dialed Daniel and Marian's number, relieved when Marian answered the phone.

"Marian, it's Taryn. I'm with Vicki. We're OK. We're in Sibiu. We have to spend the night here. We'll get back when we can, but I have no idea when that will be. We don't know why we couldn't land."

Marian told me there was a huge strike going on, and all the trains and planes were grounded. She didn't know the reason for the strike. These things happened without warning and without explanation in Romania.

When I walked back to the waiting room, the Polish couple had returned. Soon after that, someone arrived to gather all of our passports. We lined up for an enthusiastic frisking by hand. The airport employee made me remove the scrunchy from my ponytail; I suppose it had wire in it. Usually the friskers were men. I was glad to have a woman when she snapped the underwire in my bra.

Our checked luggage had to remain on the plane. Vicki and I had learned to expect the unexpected, and so we had packed pajamas and a change of clothes in our carry-on bags. I smiled, thankful I had moved the cheese out of my suitcase minutes before I checked it.

We were marched onto a bus reeking of diesel fumes. After a 45 minute winding drive, we arrived at the center of Sibiu. We were told to stay on the bus, while the Tarom official went inside the Hotel Continental. Several minutes later, she came out and waved for us all to follow. We each signed a paper at the desk in exchange for a skeleton key. Vicki and I were given separate keys to rooms side by side, but we could have insisted on staying in the same room.

"Vicki, you know, since Tarom is willing to pay for us to have our own space, and since we never get it in Bucharest –"

"Yeah, I know. You want us to have separate rooms."

We 10 passengers were marched upstairs to our rooms. Vicki's room didn't have a light bulb. The hotel clerk came back with a bulb for her, then she locked our doors from the hallway, trapping us inside. We were under house arrest. I had a fleeting fear of what would happen in case of fire. But fire seemed to be the least of our worries.

We were hostages in the heart of Romania.

It was midnight by now. Once inside my room, I started to realize how selfish and stubborn I had been. The real reason I wanted separate rooms was that I was still frustrated about having to be the responsible one where Vicki was concerned.

The personality tests we took as a team labeled me as "field marshal." Under stress, I naturally took charge and barked orders. I inherited that quality from the Patton side of my family, being related to General Blood and Guts. Since stress was the definition of life in Romania, I needed to learn a new strategy. On our team, I often took over. After all, I was more decisive, not to mention older, than Bill. I assumed that Southern gentlemen like Bill preferred women to be meek and demure, but that was not me.

When my life was stable, I quickly reverted to the category on the tests described as enthusiastic, winsome, even charming. I preferred myself that way and felt that others liked me better, too. I didn't know how to change my temperament, and I doubted it was even possible. But if I could have done it, I would have.

I often wondered if God made a mistake creating me the way I was, and if my strong personality explained why I was still single in my thirties. People often commented that they admired my ability to be myself and not try to please everyone. If only they knew how miserable I usually felt being me. I never measured up to my own standards. Perhaps that was why I criticized others whenever they made a mistake, instead of extending grace to them as God had so freely lavished on me. *God's extravagant grace.*

Suddenly the face of my good friend Bobby flashed in my mind. *I remembered.* In college, after years of relegating Jesus to the wings while I let popularity take center stage, one evening Bobby startled me by asking what was different about me. I knew what he was after. Somehow, he'd seen a glimmer of Christ through the boards I'd erected to try to hide Him. I didn't know how to explain, and besides, I felt hypocritical since I wasn't living like a follower of Christ. I said nothing, and Bobby left.

An hour later, Bobby was killed in a head-on collision. Shattered, I turned to God. I picked up a booklet on the spirit-filled life and read about the futility of living the Christian life through our own efforts. That day, I confessed my sins to God, surrendered my whole life to Him, and asked Him to take over. Rather than feeling condemned that I hadn't answered Bobby, instead I felt free of my burden of sin and deeply loved and pursued by God.

Months later, I learned what happened in the final hour of Bobby's life. After I evaded his question, he went to the football coach and asked the same thing. The coach shared the gospel; Bobby got on his knees and gave his life to Jesus, with his face wet from tears. Within 15 minutes, he was welcomed into the presence of his Savior. Bobby was truly seeking God, and he found Him; I wasn't big enough to stand in the way.

Through Bobby's death, I learned to let Christ reign in me. God didn't need to allow me to hear the rest of the story, but He did. God overwhelmed me with His grace and forgiveness, and I promised to never forget.

Oh God, is this how I thank You for Your grace—by withholding it from others? If I can't love my teammates, what does the rest matter? I got down on my knees and put my face in my hands. "Father, once again I come to You, agreeing with You that I have sinned. I confess my attitude to You. God, I'm sorry. I thank You by faith that Jesus' death on the cross was enough to cover even this sin. Thank You, Lord, for forgiving me and filling me with the Holy Spirit. I want to be directed and empowered by Him. Please love Vicki through me."

I knew I could make one situation right.

"Vicki," I called through the wall. "Can you hear me? Are you OK?"

"Yeah, I'm OK."

"Is your light working now?"

"Yeah."

"Vicki, I'm sorry I've been so critical. I don't want to be like that. Will you forgive me? And, can you bear with me? I have so many rough edges—"

"Yes, of course I forgive you," she said without a moment's hesitation. "And I'm sorry I messed things up."

"It's OK."

"Just think, Taryn. If I'd flown home on Friday, you'd be stuck here all by yourself."

Rather than being angry with me, Vicki looked on the positive, humbling me further.

"I'm glad you're here with me, Vicki. I mean that. You want to pray together?"

I put my hands on the wall separating us as the words spilled out.

"Thank You, Father, for this situation. We don't understand it, we're kind of scared, but we know that You are in control. It didn't take You by surprise. You tell us in Your Word to thank You in all situations, and so we're doing that now. Thank You for my teammate, Vicki. Help me be more loving to Vicki. Father, we love You. We come before You in the name of our risen Savior, Jesus Christ. Amen."

Vicki piped up. "And Lord, please watch over us and keep us safe. And give us good rest tonight. And bring us back to Bucharest safely. Amen."

I crawled in bed and hummed praise songs softly to myself until I drifted off. My heart felt cleansed and calm, assured of His power and presence.

February 1991, Sibiu, Romania

The pounding on my door roused me from a deep sleep. The hotel clerk called out, "Breakfast in 30 minutes."

I quickly got ready, thankful for the change of clothes we had packed. As I had suspected, my period had come in the middle of the night.

My stash of tampons from the States were all back in Bucharest. And it had been an ordeal to get that box, going to the *Vama* (Customs) office in the train station where unsavory men lined the hallway. The customs men had opened every box of tampons with their dirty fingernails. They picked up a few, twirling them quizzically, opening the wrappers.

"What is this?" the head guy asked.

"It is something personal, something for women," I said.

"What is it?" His tone became fiercer.

"It is for the cycle. For women who are on *stop*." I had listened to the way Romanian girls put it.

"What do you mean by that?"

His colleague whispered to him.

"Tell me how you use this device."

"Please, I am embarrassed to explain this. It is OK. It is not a problem. You can believe me, please. My mother sent it to me."

After fighting so hard for that precious shipment, I hoarded it safely away in Bucharest. Why would I pack it for a trip the week before I was supposed to need it?

Now, today, I had to think of a solution. I had bought 12 packs of pocket Kleenex in Prague. I would try to fashion one of them like a pad.

Romanian women had no feminine hygiene products available. They made their own pads by rolling up cotton batting, hand-washing the stained cotton each month, and hanging it up to dry and re-use next month.

This was one of the most vivid proofs to me that the Communist government didn't take care of its people. It didn't provide for the basic needs of half of its population. It didn't care that women were humiliated. It was next to impossible to find any kind of paper products. Every once in a while, toilet paper would appear on a store shelf or in a kiosk, but it was rougher than sandpaper.

When we were ushered down to breakfast, I quietly explained my problem to our younger flight attendant. Her name badge read: "Domnişoara Constantinescu." Miss Constantinescu. I guessed that she was about 20 years old. She was pretty, with long, dark hair and dark eyes. I asked her where I could find cotton batting.

"I do not live here," she said, with a gentle voice like most young Romanian women. "But I will try to find out. We talk about such personal matters, you and I, that I think that you should call me Teodora."

Our other flight attendant appeared to be past the age of having my problem, but women must stick together, so I approached her. She had salt and pepper hair severely pulled back in a bun. Her nametag read: "Doamna (Mrs.) Popescu."

"Doamna Popescu, please do not be angry with me." I'd already learned the proper way to approach a stranger. This staid woman commanded formality.

She didn't know where to find what I needed, but she asked the hotel clerk and the Tarom representative. I had no pride left. All the women in our group now understood my problem. I only hoped the men wouldn't find it out.

No one knew where I could find a remedy. It seemed the pocket Kleenex were my best solution.

I could do nothing else for now, so I settled into the seat Vicki had saved for me at the Japanese man's table. It turned out he lived in Paris, and he wanted to open a Kodak processing store, where make-up would also be sold, in downtown Bucharest. That piece of news was enough to brighten our day.

After breakfast, the woman from Tarom announced that we were going to have a tour of the fine city of Sibiu. "We show you the heart of Romania," she said.

We lined up, single file, our pilot in front, then the Tarom woman, the 10 hostages, and the two flight attendants. We climbed aboard our bus. The airport still hadn't opened, so they attempted to keep us occupied.

Sibiu was lovely. Cradled by the snow-capped Carpathian Mountains, it was an old Saxon village in the heart of Transylvania. Medieval charm oozed from the town with its colorful buildings, spires, and clock towers. The bus stopped in the center for us to get out and explore. A dusting of snow remained on the rooftops and in the trees. I pulled my scarf tighter around my neck. A February nip chilled the air. We walked to the main square, called *Piaţa Mare* (or big). From there we descended the stairway passage to arrive in *Piaţa Mica* (or small).

After living in aesthetically-challenged Bucharest, I felt proud to see that there were quaint towns in Romania. Sibiu was almost as pretty as Prague.

Our bus, with its well-worn tires, slid along the curvy roads, back to the hotel for lunch. I already felt queasy from my period. I purposely sat towards the front of the bus, hoping that would help. But it wasn't enough. With barely any warning, I jumped up and motioned to our Tarom guide to have the driver pull over. I made it out the door just in time.

This is all I need. Now I have thrown up in front of our entire bus. Embarrassed, I wanted to disappear. I stood with my back to the bus, drumming up the courage to get back on.

The women's eyes were filled with empathy.

Teodora leaned over and gently smoothed my hair. "You poor dear one. I do not stop asking and looking, but I have not found what you need."

After a large lunch and time for a siesta, we were herded together again to get back on our bus. We had to pack our bags and deposit them on the bus. Everywhere we walked, we lined up in the same order, with the pilot at the head and the flight attendants taking up the rear.

Still waiting for the airport to open, we were taken to the Brukenthal Palace downtown, now a history and art museum. After a couple hours there, we returned to the airport to wait. Tarom announced that the Otopeni airport in Bucharest hadn't opened yet, so we reboarded our bus and returned to our hotel to eat dinner and spend another night.

Vicki and I ate dinner, a much lighter meal than lunch, with the other Slavic-speaking couple. We found out they were from Prague. They were speaking Czechoslovakian.

We retired early to read and catch up in our journals. It felt good to be still, to not be careening around curves in a bus, and to have some blessed time of quiet. Back in Bucharest, Saturday mornings were the only time I could count on to be alone. I would go downtown to the Hotel Intercontinental bar with a tea bag, my journal, and letters to write. The bartenders would give me "the regular," a free cup of hot water in which to dunk my tea bag. I'd snuggle up in a wing-back chair by the window, overlooking the city below, wrapped in a few pleasant hours of solitude. I found that bars are empty at 10:00 in the morning.

It seemed my pocket Kleenex was doing the trick, just not as absorbent as the real thing. I tried to ration them to last until we made it home, but unless we flew back first thing in the morning, my supply would run out.

The next day was déja vu all over again (to mimic one of my favorite philosophers, baseball great Yogi Berra). We ate breakfast, loaded our bags, marched to our bus, and cruised the winding mountain roads. As we lined up to exit our bus for a brisk walk around the square, Teodora pulled me aside.

"Be attentive. You have spot on back of you."

I turned to look. It was true. I quickly tied my sweater around my waist to cover the spot, feeling even more humiliated. I was out of pocket Kleenex.

Once on board, the Tarom woman grabbed the microphone. She beamed.

"I have good news. Otopeni is now open!"

We cheered. Just in time.

"It is the hour for lunch at hotel. We are democracy now, so you will vote. You will have a voice. Do you choose to return to hotel to eat lunch and then go to aeroport? Or do you want to go direct to aeroport?"

The count was 6–4. Lunch won.

I thought of the long drive to the airport and longer lunches. I thought of my sweater tied around my waist.

I stood up and grabbed the mike. "Please! You all know I am sick. I need to go home right away. I beg you, please, let us vote again."

To Romanians who revel in melodrama, my actions might be considered a *spectacol*, maybe even a *scandal*. I didn't care. Some things were important enough to risk others' opinions of me.

This time the vote was 7–3, in favor of going straight to the airport. My impassioned plea had persuaded three people.

Our bus rumbled on to the airport, where we received our passports. We boarded the plane with our carry-on bags in tow and a bounce in our steps.

The propellers started turning. Teodora and Doamna Popescu strapped themselves in, facing us. Teodora smiled at me.

"We go home now," she said.

I saw our Tarom official and the Hotel Continental clerk racing toward the plane, furiously waving. The pilot came out of his cockpit and barked an order to Doamna Popescu. She got up to let the women on board.

They were speaking rapidly, gesturing frantically. It seemed that Tarom refused to pay the hotel bill for the three German businessmen. The Tarom woman tried to explain that to the Germans. They didn't understand Romanian. She couldn't speak German.

The pilot again stormed out of the cockpit. "Quiet! You women, stop the noise! *Imediat!* You give me headache. Leave me in peace! You," he pointed to Doamna Popescu, the senior flight attendant. "You take care of this problem."

He turned off the propeller and heaved himself down in his chair with an exaggerated sigh.

"Who can translate for us?" Doamna Popescu looked over all the passengers. "Does anyone speak German?" No response. "Russian?"

The Polish man said he could translate from Russian to English. One of the German men said he knew English. And so the four-way translation began.

"*Aveţi mare problema*," the Tarom woman said in Romanian.

Doamna Popescu spoke next in Russian. "*U vas bolshaya problema.*"

"You have big problem," said the Pole.

"*Wir haben ein grosses Problem,*" the German said to his friends.

After the whole situation had been translated, the German emphatically sent his answer to paying their bill back through the chain in the opposite direction. "*Nein!*" he barked.

"No!"

"*Nyet!*"

"*Nu!*"

The Germans refused to pay. I didn't know why Tarom would foot the hotel bill for the rest of us and not for the Germans, but I figured it must be something political.

The Polish man talked to the German man, begging him to pay the bill. The German relented, but only if he would get a receipt.

"I am sorry," the hotel woman said. "My receipt book is back at hotel. I will have to return to hotel to get it."

We all knew what that meant. The drive to the hotel took 45 minutes each way. Typically, when Romanians make that length of a trip at this time of day, they stay and eat lunch and maybe even nap. It would be hours before we left.

The Polish man spoke up again. "Please. The young lady." He looked at me. "She is very sick. She must go to doctor. Please, I beg you, pay bill without receipt."

The German turned and consulted with his two colleagues. Then he looked at all of us and said, "*Ja! Sehr gut.* Very good."

The plane erupted in cheers.

"This is the life in Romania," said the Pole. "I love to fly Tarom!"

We all applauded, and laughter filled the plane. "Bravo! We love Tarom!"

Vicki and I high-fived each other. We were still clapping as the propellers began to whirl and the Tarom woman and the hotel woman disembarked. Teodora and Doamna Popescu buckled their seat belts once more. Our plane started rolling down the runway.

Home. We were going home. And I sat next to my friend, Vicki. In the heart of Romania, God reminded me of His heart to make relationships right and to offer forgiveness. Even with a stain on the back of me, I felt clean.

What About You?

- Think of a time you have experienced tension with another person. Did you feel a need to ask forgiveness? What about with God? How did you feel afterward?

- Why do you think it is so difficult for us to ask forgiveness and confess our sins?

- What does it look like for a life to be empowered and directed by the Holy Spirit? Imagine how your life could be different if you lived every day surrendered to Christ's Lordship.

- If you could change one quality about your temperament, what would it be and why? How can you develop and grow in that area?

Chapter 6

GRAY BECOMES GREEN

*To all who mourn in Israel, he will give beauty for ashes,
joy instead of mourning, praise instead of despair.
For the Lord has planted them like strong and
graceful oaks for his own glory.*

—Isaiah 61:3 (NLT)

March 1991, Bucharest, Romania

SNOWDROP FLOWERS STARTED to peek shyly, like
pearls in the snow, just in time. Romanians had an all-purpose
celebration of spring, love, and women on the first day of March,
called *Mărțișor*. In spite of the cold weather, everyone held hope
that spring would soon burst forth. The cares of life seemed to
lift a little.

Vendors on every street corner sold little charms with red
and white streamers. I bought about 30 and gave them out to
my friends. I received just as many, pinning them proudly up
and down the front of my coat. Better than Valentine's Day or
Mother's Day, *Mărțișor* gave everyone a chance to honor several
people they cared about, not just mothers or sweethearts. The

honorees could be friends, teachers, or neighbors. The weeklong celebration culminated on March 8, with International Women's Day.

I had many reasons to rejoice. The Gulf War ended the day before *Mărțișor*, after just six weeks. We learned that the fighting had started on January 17 from Bill's short-wave radio. We skipped language school that day and gathered in our room to pray about the war when the embassy staff came to warn us that we could be a target. They said that any citizen of a country at war is at risk as an expatriate. We lived in a dorm with many students from the Middle East, some even from Iraq. The embassy officials cautioned us to be careful.

I also celebrated the fact that my parents had written back, giving their blessings for me to stay on longer in Romania. My father, a man of few words, was pleased that I wanted to know his opinion. He wrote, "If you feel that God is leading you to do this, then go for it. Where better can a person be but in the center of God's will? If you don't go, then you might regret it the rest of your life. I am concerned at times for your safety and comfort, but I don't fret and lay awake at night, because I know that God is in charge. We gave you over to Him to take care of you years ago."

Mom wrote, "If you're sure that God is leading you, then that's enough for me. Knowing you as I do and reading your letters about how much you love Romania, I would have been surprised if you had not wanted to stay and give it a go. I love you and I will miss you, but I realize that laborers are needed." My course had been set.

The bleak, gray world turned vibrant overnight with the coming of spring. Brilliant flowers and green grass that had been forming in the darkness burst forth on the tired world one April morning. In the blink of an eye, everything was transformed. I had never appreciated the color green before as I did that spring.

I drank in the lush color with all my senses, even tasting the freshness. I felt alive.

The fleecy winter hats began to come off, that is, except on the children. Their heads were always covered up, and not just babies. Romanians proudly pointed out that their children never had ear infections. Maybe they were on to something.

Every day, an enterprising man delivered bread to us foreigners in the dorms. We nicknamed him *The Pâine Man.* One day in April, he took off his fleecy hat, and his hair underneath startled me. It looked identical to his hat. His dark curls bore the shape of a cylindrical fez.

The coming of Easter, a more significant holy day than Christmas in Orthodox countries, harkened spring's arrival. For weeks before Easter, every stranger who greeted me on the streets or over the phone said, *"Isus a înviat,"* or Jesus rose. I learned to respond, *"Adevărat a înviat."* Truly He rose. In public, without fear, words about Jesus were spoken aloud in a country where His name had only been whispered for 45 years.

Friends invited Vicki and me to a monastery outside of Bucharest for a midnight mass on Easter Eve. We joined a huge throng, walking up a hill and past a lake and ancient graveyard. The round church was adorned with beautiful frescoes on the outside walls. The long-bearded priests carried bells and chanted soulful music. They glided by, wearing stiff hats and black cassocks that cascaded onto the ground. The sky twinkled with stars, illuminating the tiny buds ready to burst out of their wintry graves. We all held small white tapers, lit from the priest's large candle at midnight. The final words "Jesus rose!" and a bell's deep chime echoed in the stillness. The night was sacred. Joy replaced despair.

After the mass, we returned to our friend's apartment for more celebrating. A bowl of solid red eggs sat on the coffee table, next to a vase of pussy willows. We tasted the sweet Easter cake and sipped red wine, then said "Jesus rose" and broke an egg on the forehead of the person next to us. As we tapped egg to brow, we said *"Pac! Pac!"* The roles switched with an egg broken on the originator's forehead with the words "Truly He rose. *Pac! Pac!"* I was thankful the eggs were hard-boiled. We stayed up until the sun rose with this wild egg-breaking party, being watchful all night long.

A few hours later, the four of us on my team had dressed for church and arrived to a building already packed. As usual, the usher escorted us to the front row, giving foreigners an undeserved seat of honor. After about 10 minutes, the sermon finished and everyone stood to kiss each other. I thought the service would continue after this greeting. But it had ended. Several of our students made their way to us, laughing. We didn't know that Daylight Savings Time started that morning, and so we arrived one hour late. I missed my first Easter sermon in Romania.

That week, the airports and train stations closed once again. This time we found out why. The exiled King Mihai had tried to return. I learned that he had also attempted to enter the country at Christmas, and again in February, the reason we were stranded in Bucharest and held hostage in Sibiu. The new government, concerned about Mihai's uncontrolled popularity, used their heavy-handed tactics to prohibit him from getting in.

Mihai became king in 1927, at the tender age of six. He "reigned" for three years until his father returned with his commoner mistress to take over. Crowned again at the age of 19, Mihai ruled during World War II. Romania had sided with Germany and committed its own horrible atrocities against the Jews. Young Mihai led a coup against the pro-Nazi Iron Guard leader, Antonescu, and changed Romania's allegiance to the Allies in the middle of the war. In 1947, the Soviets rolled in and forced Mihai to abdicate and take exile in Switzerland. He married Princess Anne from France, and they had five daughters, all raised in Switzerland, yet loyal to their Romanian heritage.

King Mihai had never returned to the country he loved. The people adored him for his courage and character. Many were vocal about wanting the monarchy to return. Romania had only had royalty for 66 years. In 1881, during a desperate time in Romania's history, Prince Charles of the Hohenzollern family was imported from Germany to become Romania's King Carol I. The family motto, *Nihil Sine Deo*, means "Nothing Without God." That sounded better to me than the Communist idea that God does not exist, or Karl Marx's statement that "Religion is the opium of the people."

The number of students who trusted Christ continued to grow. By April, I met weekly with three groups of girls who were taking big steps in their new relationships with Christ. One group included English language majors whom I met with downtown in their faculty at the University. These girls were some of the top students in the country, and they lived in their parents' flats in Bucharest. I met with the other groups in their rooms in the Polytechnic dorms next to mine. They came from other towns throughout Romania. Noemi was an ethnic Hungarian from Transylvania, a minority in the city of Bucharest.

Several students had trouble pronouncing my name, Taryn. Girls' names in Romania were feminine versions of the boys' names and ended in the letter "a." The name Daniel morphed into Daniela for a girl, and Mihai became Mihaela.

I had just learned a word similar to my name. It was "*teren,*" and it meant ground or field. I suggested that friends add an "a" and call me "Terena." It stuck, and soon Terena became my Romanian name.

Now I had a new name as well as a new birth year.

My Bible study students began to get an inkling that I had other Romanian friends besides them. They were almost jealous to know that I spent as much time with other people as I did with them. They needed to understand why.

One of my Bible study groups in Bucharest.

We were becoming more open all the time about our identity, that it could be more than a coincidence that we all happened to be Christians from America. The time had come to hold our first big public meeting and invite the students we met with regularly. We reserved a room on campus and planned skits and icebreakers. Daniel would give a message on God's love and forgiveness.

I walked over to the big event with Cristina, Tereza, Violeta, Ofelia, and Noemi. At first, there were not many people inside. Romanians have a more relaxed attitude toward time than Americans do, so I tried not to panic. As we chatted, the room kept filling up. When Daniel started speaking, we counted over 100 students—all in one room. The year before, it would have been illegal for groups a fraction this size to meet together in the same room.

After the meeting, Noemi and I talked with several colleagues from her faculty. They had questions about the topic. Noemi explained to them how she came to believe that God loved her, but her sins formed a wall that separated her from Him. Jesus Christ paid the penalty for her sins through His death on the cross, and He bridged that wall. She went on to say that knowing that intellectually wasn't enough. It was up to her whether she'd accept the free gift that Jesus offered. She chose to accept it, and now her life had purpose. Noemi told her classmates that Jesus loved them too, and He offered them new life, asking if they wanted to invite Him into their hearts. Three of those students said they did, and Noemi led them in a prayer right there, outside our meeting room, in view of everyone.

I had not intentionally trained Noemi in how to do that. I had modeled it for her, but we had never shared our faith together, as I had done with the students I discipled in the States. It was the most natural thing in the world for her to tell others about the greatest gift she had ever received.

"I'm so proud of you! You were so bold to tell your friends about Jesus," I said to Noemi later.

She looked puzzled. "Why would I keep that to myself?"

As the school year wound to an end, students geared up for a month of comprehensive exams, regurgitating everything they'd learned to date in their college career. I prepared to leave for the States a few months earlier than my teammates, transitioning to my long-term assignment by seeing my family, raising more financial support, and going through intensive cross-cultural training.

Bill, Dan, Vicki, and I had our farewell meal together in the Athenee Palace Hotel. For old time's sake, we found a *Securitate* microphone hidden in the vase of flowers on our table. Just like our first meal together in Vienna, we laughed, even harder this time. We prayed for each other, thanking God for what He had done in and through us that year.

God had answered my plea from Vienna. He had proved Himself faithful and provided all the grace and strength we needed. He had blessed our feeble efforts and drawn many people to Himself. It had been a good year.

The four of us had shared experiences together that we were certain no one else would ever be able to relate to or fully understand. We had gotten on each other's nerves, but we were closer than brothers and sisters, living in tight quarters and intense situations with no break. Now that was ending. I loved them, and they would not be there when I returned.

We four had certainly seen the very best and the very worst about each other. We focused so much on understanding the new culture we lived in that we lost patience with our own. Our mantra for understanding Romanians was, "It's not wrong; it's just different." However, we often treated each other as though we believed, "That's just plain wrong."

All of our emotional energy had gone into surviving. There had been nothing left over to keep up the façades we were accustomed to hiding behind in the States, so we were real all of the time. We let it all hang out—the ugly and the grand. Our fears, our moments of trust, our hurts, the little glimmers of God's image revealed in us, our selfish moments, and our triumphs were all exposed.

I had finally learned to go to Wendy and Marian, women close to my age, with how I was doing emotionally and not burden my younger team. Together, Wendy and Marian made up my composite best friend. I had deep soul-level conversations with Wendy once a week where I felt totally understood, and lighter ones punctuated with lots of laughter with Marian every day or so. Thankfully, they would both be there when I came back.

June 1991, New York City

The trip home was long. I couldn't get my last image from the train station in Bucharest out of my mind. Each time I closed my eyes, the sea of white handkerchiefs waved by my Romanian friends re-appeared, zooming out to a small white dot on the horizon before disappearing.

I flew in to New York on a gorgeous, clear day. Looking down, I saw the Statue of Liberty proudly raising her welcoming flame and choked back a sob. I felt like an immigrant seeing that grand lady for the very first time. Soon I would touch my feet on the land of the free. I'd tasted life without much freedom, and I was glad to be home. I studied the skyline of Manhattan from my airplane window, recognizing the World Trade Center towers, the Empire State building, and the Brooklyn Bridge.

As I deplaned to go through customs, I overheard several foreigners who were confused about which line to join. I guided a few people to their lines and pointed it out to others. After struggling myself as a foreigner trying to speak a new language, I could relate to what they were experiencing, and I wanted to help.

As I walked through JFK airport to find my new gate to Baltimore, I felt self-conscious. I had worn the same few outfits, with their permanent dusty appearance, for the last 10 months. I hadn't cut my hair once. I knew I looked dowdy and out of style. As I listened to the excited American chatter, I realized I didn't fit. I wondered if everyone else noticed.

When I stepped off the plane in Baltimore, my parents met me with a box of peppermint patties, just what I'd been craving, and a clock shaped like a piece of bread. My father had called the Romanian Embassy in Washington to ask how to say "Welcome Home," and then painted *"Bine aţi venit"* on the face of my clock.

I had been warned that people might not be interested in the dramatic things that had happened in my life. Fortunately, for the most part, my friends and family were fascinated. I had a great time visiting my ministry partners all over the country. These people were so much more than financial backers; they were my faithful prayer warriors and dear friends. It took no effort at all to raise the additional support I needed for the next several years. I just sent out one letter, and the money poured in. Within a few weeks, I had everything I needed.

I had returned home, but it felt like a strange new world. Wal-Marts enthralled me. I loved getting free refills on sodas and standing in quick-moving, straight lines. I forgot that water was available at any time and still only showered or washed dishes at night. In the mornings, I would lie in bed and listen in vain for the rhythmical sounds I had grown accustomed to, horses clomping on their way to market and women beating their rugs.

I felt critical of my culture, and I didn't enjoy feeling that way. At lunch one day, I counted a friend throwing out six paper towels after drying lettuce leaves, and remembered rationing squares of toilet paper. When I called old friends to get together, they would schedule me three weeks in advance for a one-hour lunch and rush off to their next appointment. In Romania, friends would drop everything to spend all day with me. I struggled with the shallowness, waste, and excess. I loved and missed America when I was away, and yet now I felt out of place. If I voiced anything negative, I felt judged.

I remembered the propaganda film I caught in a Romanian dorm, showing the worst about America. I had expected the footage I saw of homeless people, drunks sleeping on park benches, and elderly people living in institutions rather than with their families. What surprised me were the images of mansions and jet setters. I assumed Americans' wealth would be something to hide, because it might make people want to defect. Instead, it sickened Romanians that we had citizens unwilling to share their bounty with others.

When my three-month cross-cultural training began, I felt free to express my conflicting emotions. I was with others who had experienced the adjustment of returning home and being misunderstood. Besides classes, my training included living in the African American community in Bakersfield, being part of an African Methodist Episcopal church, and doing ministry in the projects. I learned how to take timeless spiritual principles and explain them within the context of a different culture within my own country. I had never before shared the gospel with someone like Ruby, who was handcuffed and hauled off by parole officers before she could answer if she wanted Jesus in her life.

After Bakersfield, I saw Max and found that my feelings for him were not completely dead yet, although I knew he wasn't right for me. He tried to force his foot in the door that I pushed closed with all my might. Since my heart was so fickle, I knew I needed to keep time and space between Max and me.

Before I had moved from Berkeley to Romania, a guy friend from my church had offered to store my things in his garage. It had been an answer to a specific need at that time. The first day I had attended that church, I noticed Steve from across the room. His dark good looks were striking. I floated when he called me that same day for a date. We got to know each other through group events, and Steve told me he was interested in a serious relationship with me. I felt drawn to him, but I also sensed God tugging at my heart to move to Eastern Europe. As much as I admired Steve's kindness and character, I had to tell him that I didn't see any future for us since we were headed in opposite directions. Steve still needed to heal from his wife abandoning him a few years before. His two young children were his priority, and I was ill-prepared at the age of 28 to grapple with issues like divorce and remarriage. My respect for Steve grew when he didn't let my rejection stop him from becoming a good friend.

Now that I was going away for much longer, I decided to move my things from Steve's garage to a storage unit near my brother in Arizona. It made sense to me to have family watch over my things. I spent a day at Steve's, weeding through my belongings once more, finding more to donate or ship to

Romania, and catching up with my friend and ministry partner. Steve and I loaded the few nicer pieces of furniture I had, along with all my photo albums, into a truck bound for Phoenix.

During my months back in the States, dramatic events kept unfolding in my adopted land. The USSR staged a coup in August 1991, overthrowing Gorbachev. Four months later, on Christmas Day, the once-powerful Soviet Union had officially dissolved. All 15 republics declared their independence from Mother Russia. West and East Germany had reunified the year before. Even the country of Albania, in the Eastern Bloc, was now free.

After Thanksgiving and Christmas with family, my time to leave had come. I cherished having the month to play with my nephew, Mark, now an adorable toddler, and his four-year-old brother, Alex. My sister-in-law, Susie, was expecting a baby girl. It hurt knowing I would miss watching the kids grow up. I sobbed at the airport when I said good-bye to my brother, and later my parents.

"It feels like I'll never see you again," my brother said to me. This time, I was not embarking on a fun adventure. I knew first-hand how difficult and frightening my life would be. It would be several more years before I could return home. It felt final.

I also knew I'd never fit in again, anywhere. I'd been in Romania long enough to learn that there I'm defined as an American, and I'll never get beyond that. In America, my values had already changed. I no longer felt like a real American, but I wasn't a Romanian either. I guessed I had become an American-European.

I made a decision that whenever I feel lonely or misunderstood, rather than feel sorry for myself, I will give thanks that I'm a citizen of heaven. I'm not supposed to feel comfortable anywhere on earth, because this is not my final home. I'm only passing through.

Whether I'd be in Romania for three more years, seven, ten, or for the rest of my life—I was making a commitment to stay until the cloud moved. I'd be there until God called me to leave and go on to my next assignment.

January 1992, Bucharest, Romania

I arrived back in Romania in the middle of a blizzard. The sparkling snow made Bucharest look beautiful and at peace. But it didn't last long. Soon the piled-up snow beside the roads turned black. I discovered that September is a much more pleasant time of year to arrive than January. After seven months in the States, I had forgotten the effect living in a colorless and drab world had on me. I knew from experience that it would remain gray for several months.

My second year in Romania started differently, mostly because I lived like an adult—in a flat and not a dorm room. I had stuffed my two suitcases in the States with things to make my place feel more like home, and even shipped over some boxes of artwork, home fabrics, and books. I knew I needed to make a haven to be able to thrive for the long haul.

My landlady, Doamna Andrescu, worked for the state telephone company and installed a hard-to-get telephone in my apartment. We had mail slots in the lobby, and my family and a few close friends had my address. My mother numbered her letters to me, and I figured that about seven out of 10 actually made it. When my niece, Lisa, was born in February, someone reached their hand inside my mail slot, stole her baby pictures, and put the opened envelope back. *How could anyone be that cruel?*

I continued going to language class every morning, picking up where I'd left off the spring before. I struggled to stay focused on my homework since I didn't have a roommate to keep me accountable. Seven new Americans had joined our team of six,

101

making it three singles and five couples. We even had two children and a brand new baby on the team now. All the staff had moved out of the dorms, but most lived in another part of the city from me. I often visited them on my way home from language class.

When I approached my apartment lobby those first few months, any neighbors who were there would quickly scurry behind their doors, like roaches scattering when I turned on the light. I realized that they were afraid of me. In the past, if they ever talked to a foreigner, they would have to voluntarily go to the police to be interrogated, or risk being reported and perhaps even going to jail. It took time for people to get past those memories. I determined to do my best to be friendly and ease their fears. I hoped to win them over in the months ahead.

Every apartment building had an informant who lived in the lobby, recording everyone who came and left, with the exact times. A team from Singapore came to help us with ministry and left my flat carrying their suitcases.

The informant quickly called my landlady. "The American girl is having wild parties. The Chinese have stolen your television and toaster."

Doamna Andrescu called me and asked me to meet her in the lobby. "That woman!" she said. "She doesn't know it's 1992. She thinks it's still 1984." I followed her as she marched inside the informant's apartment.

I saw what she meant about 1984. The stool and pad of paper set up next to the giant magnifying peephole reminded me of Big Brother, watching everyone, everywhere, all the time.

"This is a good girl and I trust her," Doamna Andrescu said, touching my head. "Please do not accuse her of stealing from me ever again."

Romanians kept their flats immaculate. With such small spaces, their belongings had to be tidy. The women took pride in their homes and worked hard to keep them neat. It was customary to remove your shoes as soon as you entered and put on slippers from the basket inside the door. Mud constantly covered the backs of everyone's legs, kicked up as we trudged along the sidewalks swimming in the stuff. Women aired out their bedding over the balcony every morning before they left for work and scrubbed the floors on their hands and knees each night. It was impossible to keep anything clean for more than a few days. Because of the coal heat and pollution, a thick layer of black dust would reappear daily on the furniture. White clothes permanently appeared a dingy gray.

The outside of the apartment blocks was another story. They didn't belong to anyone; only to the State. No one cared what they looked like. The streets were filthy and so were the buildings. During the early days of Communism, whole villages were destroyed and the peasants forced to move to Bucharest for the good of the State. People who lived in thatched-roof huts without electricity and plumbing were herded like cattle into skyscraper apartments. They retained their village ways. At night, I would come home to see men lined up, peeing in the

Outside my apartment building in Bucharest.

103

bushes outside my building. Sometimes I felt like screaming, "Zip up!" or pelting them with tomatoes from my balcony above, but I never did.

A bread line, seen from my apartment window.

One March night about 3:00, I awoke to pounding at my door. I pulled on my robe as I walked toward it. A man yelled, "*Poliția!* Open up!" I looked through the peephole, but the hallway was too dark to see. I cracked the door open, with the security chain keeping it in check. Several men were standing at the threshold. As I held my hand on the knob, they kicked the door open, breaking the chain, and charged in. A policeman in plain clothes, one in a uniform, and two military guys with machine guns had stormed into my apartment. My blood turned cold.

The plainclothes policeman grabbed the neck of my bathrobe and yelled that I needed to turn over Andrei Andrescu, my landlady's son. He assumed I lived there with him. His breath reeked of alcohol. I knocked his hand away and screamed, "*Lasați-mă în pace!*" (Leave me in peace). He wanted me to go into the bedrooms with him as he searched for Andrei. I refused; I guessed what he had in mind. I stood by the open door, where I felt safest, insisting that the men with guns stay in the hallway.

After turning over furniture, searching every room, and barking orders for probably 15 minutes, the police left. I pushed a table in front of the door to barricade it, shaken.

I was too scared to sleep, and so I just sat up in my bed, with all the lights on, listening to praise music. I shivered under my bundle of blankets and planned what I should do.

As soon as the sun came up, I called Doamna Andrescu to come fix my door, and I told her that the police were looking for Andrei. Then I headed to the American Consulate to file a report.

The people there were very sympathetic. I felt comforted. I asked if I did the right thing. In America, when the police come to your door, you have to let them in. I didn't want to be foolish here.

The embassy staff told me that even with the lack of freedoms in Romania, the police needed a search warrant and were not supposed to drink on the job. They asked me for names. Naturally, none of these officers had name badges.

When I returned home, neighbors who had never spoken to me before came by with home-baked breads and flowers. The women gently touched my cheek and looked into my eyes with compassion. No one mentioned the night before, but I knew they had heard the ruckus, and they were expressing their care to me. They were no longer afraid of me.

I arrived late to language class that day. I thought about skipping but decided I needed to be with my friends. I explained the whole story in Romanian to my class. My teacher was proud of me for standing firm and correctly using the very Romanian phrase, "Leave me in peace!"

I didn't want to be alone. That day I adopted one of my teammate's kittens, a beautiful jet black girl. A few days later, my good friend Corina moved in with me. I didn't have to ask her. When she heard my story, she said, "Terena, I come now."

We had already discussed her coming eventually to help me with language and teach me more about the culture. Corina and I watched Romanian television together, played Scrabble in Romanian, and laughed a lot. My family grew.

Once again, green appeared overnight in April, and it stunned me. I had survived my second winter in Romania. My difficulties felt light somehow, and my soul experienced spring.

This Easter in 1992 was a historic one. We celebrated, freely once more, the fact that Jesus rose. And we cheered for someone else who had returned to life. King Mihai came home to Romania, the first time since his exile 45 years earlier. People thronged the streets for his procession, throwing flowers and confetti, blowing horns and rejoicing.

The long, gray winter seemed to be ending.

What About You?

- Think of a time when your life was like a long, gray winter. How did you feel? How did you respond when things brightened for a season?

- Think about Noemi's statement about her faith in Christ. "Why would I keep that to myself?" How can you give your faith away?

- Have you ever felt as if you don't fit in anywhere—with no one to relate to or understand you? How have you handled that?

- If you had a composite best friend, which people would fill that role? Which qualities would you want from each of them?

Chapter 7

TRANSYLVANIA

*Unless the Lord builds the house, they labor in vain who
build it; unless the Lord guards the city, the
watchman keeps awake in vain.*

—Psalm 127:1

July 1993, Cluj-Napoca, Romania

I MOVED TO Transylvania on the Fourth of July. Usually
invigorated by change, I had no idea what to expect with this
one. I hoped to build roots and a sense of family.

Cluj, the capital of Dracula's land of Transylvania, was the
first city to which our Bucharest ministry expanded. Three of
us were the first staff to leave the nest—me and a young couple,
David and Susan, who were expecting their first baby. The
ministry in Cluj had been started 10 months earlier by a Stint
team, and four of them planned to stay on to help us.

Susan and I deplaned, frazzled after listening to my cat,
LaToya, howl the whole way. David met us and dropped me
at my temporary home next to Tailors' Tower, a fragment that
remained of the old city wall. LaToya, traumatized after being

stuffed into a box on my lap for the flight, immediately shimmied into a hole under the bathtub and spent several hours hidden inside. When she padded out to explore, she found me on the balcony. I sat there with my cat on my lap, hypnotized by the full moon over the ancient wall. *I think I will like Cluj.*

All summer, I propped open the balcony door for the breeze. It also enlarged my tiny studio apartment. LaToya loved to leap from my balcony, three floors up, to the neighbor's.

One morning, I woke up with LaToya curled on the foot of my bed and two green beans on my pillow. I could not guess how they had gotten there. That day I chatted with my neighbor, Elena, in the hallway.

"Your cat sleeps with me every night," Elena said.

"That's interesting," I said. "She's here when I go to sleep and here when I wake up."

"But she's with me in the middle of the night."

It turned out that my nocturnal cat roamed freely throughout the night. The slinky black feline prowled about undetected.

Once, I returned from the *piaţa* and found LaToya pirouetting after a bird inside my apartment. I didn't want to witness the massacre, but I wanted her to be the wild animal God had created her to be. So I closed the door and left for more errands. When I came back, the dead bird had been neatly laid inside the door for me. I swept it into a dustpan with my eyes closed, and tossed it over the balcony.

Another morning, I awoke to a sharp rapping on my door. Elena stood there, frantic.

"Your cat stole my diamond ring."

"Don't worry. We will find it," I said. I searched all over my balcony and studio, then looked on the ground underneath our balconies. I found nothing.

I hurried to Elena's and asked if I could help her check her flat. As my anxiety level rose, I spied something glistening on her balcony railing. The ring was precariously perched on the

edge. My cat burglar must have dropped it out of her mouth when she made her midnight raid.

At the end of the summer, we took the students involved in our ministry to a mountain retreat, kicking off the new school year. Our destination, Padiş, was so remote that the bus only made the trek twice a week. Our mountaintop experience would last 10 days.

In the daytime, we taught basic ministry skills, and at night, we showed the *Jesus* film outside by generator, on bed sheets strung up like a screen. Hungarians, Romanians, Yugoslavs, and gypsies camped on those peaks. After the film, we talked around a campfire. Sometimes people would charm us with their national dances. The night air turned quite chilly when we returned to camp well after midnight.

We figured that one cow had been sacrificed for our meals in Padiş. We ate cow flank, ribs, liver, kidney, tongue, stomach, and eyes. I passed on the eyes.

The guys thought they had the worst housing situation, because pigs would tromp freely through their room, nuzzling them in their sleep. We girls were convinced we had it rougher. There were 15 of us, sleeping in seven twin beds pushed together. I slept on the far edge and hung on tight. Ramona, in the middle, managed a bed to herself, rolling one way and then the other, pushing each neighbor away. The girl next to me cuddled up close. It didn't seem appropriate to face her, so I never moved. For 10 days, I couldn't turn my head to the right because of my stiff neck.

When we invited the girls to this retreat, they all said, "If I don't have my period, I will go." I understood their concern. There were no bathrooms. A few holes had been dug in the ground with lean-tos providing a semblance of privacy, but it smelled so rank that we usually went elsewhere. In the daytime, I spied a cow behind the makeshift wall. We had to walk quite a distance to find a new bush to take care of business, hoping that no one would spot us.

Halfway through the time, we girls wandered down to a cold mountain stream with about six inches of water to bathe. It helped to know that everyone else felt as dirty as I did. We could do nothing to fix the situation.

Late at night after the last bi-weekly bus left, I stumbled out to the hole-in-the-ground, too sleepy to hunt for a fresh bush. I trudged behind the partition marked *Femei* for women. As I started to squat, my foot slid on something a cow had left behind. I grabbed at the rough planks to try to keep my foot from going under. The contents of the hole had a life of its own, like quicksand in a Tarzan movie. It quickly pulled my foot in, halfway up my calf. Splinters covered my hands as I finally managed to yank my leg out before it reached my knee. I yelled the only appropriate utterance for the situation. That night, the word "Crap!" reverberated from peak to peak in the Transylvanian Alps.

I staggered down to the creek where I had spied water buffalo earlier, stuck my entire leg in, and swirled the water around. Because of the cold, I had on all the clothes and socks that I had brought. I had nothing left to wear. That night, and for two nights following, I had to sleep with my wet, smelly jeans and socks. My sneakers never dried out. When I took a step, muddy-looking water squirted out.

For months afterward, I shuddered whenever I remembered the moment I fell in the hole. Legend has it that on a certain night every August, high up in the Carpathian Mountains, the word "Crap" can still be heard.

I had one year under my belt of doing ministry entirely in the Romanian language before I moved to Cluj. Now I had to revert to ministering partly in English for the Stint team and the Hungarian students, and partly in Romanian. I didn't feel ready to go backwards.

A cow in the women's outhouse (Femei) at our moutaintop retreat.

Then again, I hadn't felt ready to graduate from language class and begin to do ministry full-time in Bucharest the year before. My professors were convinced I could do it. By then, the government had legally recognized Campus Crusade, pushing me out from behind my cover as an Art History student.

My swan song essay in class had been about the 1992 Summer Olympics, entitled *Zece, Lavinia!* (Ten, Lavinia). When Lavinia Lipă from Romania received a perfect score of 10 for the gold medal in gymnastics, the television commentator screamed, "*Bravo, Lavinia! Zece, Lavinia!*" My apartment block swayed, and I heard a thunderous noise overhead. People all over Bucharest cheered, stomping their feet in their flats and blowing their car horns outside. At that moment, the entire country watched the same sports event and rejoiced as one.

111

That 1992–1993 school year, I taught in Romanian at student meetings in Bucharest, trained a new staff woman named Doina, and led training sessions for our six brand new staff—the first Romanian nationals to join our team. The first time Doina and I met Cristina, one of the students who trusted Christ with us, she praised me for speaking "very good Romanian."

After Doina talked, Cristina said, "You speak good Romanian, too."

"I am Romanian," Doina said.

I'll never forget when language clicked for me. One topic demanded to be discussed that evening. Every conversation in the dorms turned to the fire the night before that had killed four girls. I listened and helped them process the tragedy. Life and death issues became real. Late that night at home, I reflected on the conversations and realized that I hadn't translated word for word in my mind. The girls said something, and I just knew what they said. It happened automatically.

When the time had come for me to move to Cluj, I took my leave of everyone I knew. I said good-bye to the vendors in the kiosks and *piaţa*, the lady who gave me free flowers each evening, and my neighbors. In the 18 months I had lived in that apartment, I had won the neighbors over. They were no longer afraid of me. They smothered me with kisses and said I was "one in a million."

A lovely city rimmed by the Carpathian Mountains, Cluj had a more relaxed and friendly feeling than the larger Bucharest. The pace of life and speed of speaking slowed significantly. Cluj-Napoca had many names. Romanians called it Cluj, Hungarians referred to it as Kolozsvár, Germans used Klausenburg, the Latin name was Claudiopolis, and the Roman one Napoca. The region of Transylvania had bounced among Dacians, Romans, Hungarians, German Saxons, Ottomon Turks, and Austrian Habsburgs. After World War I, it was ceded to Romania.

112

Cluj's ethnic mix of Romanians and Hungarians was evident everywhere. Two huge churches, one being Hungarian Catholic and the other Romanian Orthodox, dominated the city center. The University, named Babeş-Bolyai for the Romanian scientist Babeş and Hungarian mathematician Bolyai, taught in both languages. Many of the shops downtown were run by Hungarians, noted to be better business people than Romanians and less reserved. These stores were lively with laughter, an unusual sound in Bucharest, spilling out.

I frequented the castle of Transylvania's most famous resident, Dracula, in the village of Bran at the Wallachian border. Irish author Bram Stoker took a historical figure, Vlăd Ţepeş, out of the fifteenth century and plopped him down 400 years later in his fictional novel. Vlăd was a medieval prince of sorts, but not a count. His enemies called him Dracula (Son of the Devil) or Vlăd the Impaler. At night, the gothic stronghold, set on a craggy peak with bats circling overhead, is an eerie sight. Legend has it that Dracula impaled thousands of men on tall stakes encircling his fortress, letting their blood drain to the ground. Thus, Stoker transformed him into a vampire bat, sucking blood from his victims' necks.

Romanians were ashamed to be identified with madmen like Dracula and Ceauşescu, when they could offer instead the poet Eminescu, sculptor Brâncuşi, or athletes Nadia Comenici and Ilie Năstase.

I needed coffee. I had moved into my new flat, overlooking the Someş River and Central Park, the day before. I couldn't figure out how to light the burner on my antique, mint green stove. I leaned in closer to investigate.

Pow! The explosion threw me against the far wall. Dazed, my ears rang. I patted my arms and legs. They were still attached. The sickening odor left a rotten egg taste in my mouth. Snapping to, I quickly turned off the gas.

That's when I caught the first glimpse of my face. My blackened forehead appeared larger than it used to be. The top row of my eyebrows had vanished. My hairline receded. Orange corkscrew curls dotted my forehead. I touched one and it snapped off.

I dialed David and Susan's number. "Come quick! Bring burn ointment and a camera. And coffee."

After being doctored up and photographed, I seemed none the worse for wear. Classes were starting next week, and I only had a few days to settle in. I crossed the river and walked to the lone appliance store in town to purchase a washing machine. The decision came easily since they only had one model. Stores didn't deliver merchandise, so I was on my own to find a way to get the washing machine into my flat.

Within minutes of walking to the street corner, I had flagged down a chivalrous stranger who agreed to take time out of his schedule, load my heavy machine into his truck, and drive it the few blocks to my street. Once we arrived, I found another man willing to help him carry it up and place it in my bathroom. They even hooked it up to the water source for me. I tried to give these men some money for their effort, but both emphatically resisted. At least I'd already placed some bills in the front seat of the truck.

After a few years of washing clothes by hand, I couldn't wait to use my new machine, which fit about a third of the amount as the American models. I stuffed it full and turned it on, hovering over it like an anxious mother for about 10 minutes. In Romania, only cold water enters, and it's heated inside the machine. Each cycle lasts a couple of hours. I decided I didn't need to stand there for that long, so I left to unpack more boxes.

A few minutes later, I smelled something burning. *It must be residue from this morning's oven explosion.* As I passed from the kitchen to the living room, a bright-colored movement inside the machine caught my eye.

Flames! My washing machine was on fire. I opened the front window of the machine and doused the flames. Apparently, my brand-new machine was defective. The water had failed to come in, and the clothes were heated to boiling without water.

Everything inside had turned to ashes. All my underwear from the States had disintegrated. My pillowcases that matched the duvet cover I'd sewn were gone. I cried, aware that someday I might laugh about this.

I needed to replace my underwear. I walked to the *piaţa,* where I had spotted bras the other day, wedged between cucumbers and motor oil. The woman selling them asked my size. I didn't know. The numbering system was different. She held various bras up to me, plastering them against my body, for the whole world to watch and give their opinion.

"This is too big for you," she said.

"I think this one is too tight. See, right there," said her neighbor.

Finally they settled on the right one. It was size 100. It had been an eventful first day.

We established the ministry in Cluj on a foundation of prayer. Before the school year began, our team spent many days praying together. Stinters Rob, Paul, Suzy, and Kelly joined David, Susan, and me. As one, we entreated God to be the One to build this movement. We did not want to labor in vain.

Each week, we had a prayer meeting with the students. Although we had reserved a room on campus, its door was always locked, with huge chains strung across it. The bottom pane of the glass door had been broken out. We crawled through, one at a time. The lights didn't work and neither did the heat. We stood in a large circle, hand in hand, and worshipped God together. We sang songs of praise and begged Him to work on our campus. The next week, even more students turned out to pray in that same cold room.

My team in Cluj (L–R: Rob, Kelly, Paul, Suzy, Susan, David).

We hosted all-night prayer meetings with the students, too, praying until breakfast the next morning. These meetings were as well attended as the hour-long fellowship meetings. Most of the students who came were involved in small Bible study groups that met weekly. Students in Romania didn't shy away from commitment.

We took a few breaks during the prayer nights. Several of us would pick up pizza-to-go for dinner, a new concept that thrilled us Americans. The topping left something to be desired, however. The pizza-maker would fill an empty beer can with ketchup for us to pour over the thin cheese pizza.

The second semester, we stepped up to having our prayer meetings in a dorm on the thirteenth floor, with no elevator. Arriving out of breath, we prayed in a room where five of our male students lived. Guys' and girls' rooms in Romania were equally tidy. As I looked at the tightly-made beds and neatly-stacked papers, I remembered with horror how American guys kept their dorm rooms.

The other foundation for our group in Cluj was love, the kind that defies logic, which only God can give. Our team truly cared for each other. We were like family. Our fun and friendships were contagious. We saw Hungarian and Romanian students transcend the ancient cultural strife and love each other, demonstrating their faith in Christ to be real and growing. That was unheard of.

Our ministry countrywide aimed to show the *Jesus* film in every village in Romania. Teams of nationals were trained and sent out to do this. Romanians presented the *Jesus* film in gypsy villages and discipled new believers. Hungarians did the same in Romanian villages. Already, scores of new churches had been planted and taken root. These believers rose above their prejudices to share God's love with people they had once looked down on. I had never experienced unity like this before.

The whole city buzzed with the news. A taxi driver had been killed in his cab the night before. It was the first murder anyone had heard of in Cluj, at least the first slaying by a regular citizen and not the former government.

The day of the burial, the city screeched to a halt. All shops and businesses closed. Everyone dressed in black and filled the sidewalks for the funeral procession. The widow and children walked behind the horse-drawn hearse. Every taxi in the victim's company crawled by next, followed by the other taxi fleets in town. The police cars and other relatives in regular Dacias took up the rear.

I witnessed a city shocked by violence. I thought of taxi drivers in the States, every night climbing into their cab and wondering whether it might be their last. I remembered our news being filled with tales of murder. *We must be desensitized to violence.* It felt good to be horrified.

And yet at the cinema, Romanians didn't know how to react. They laughed when someone was killed on screen. I don't think they meant to be callous. They probably thought it was supposed to be slapstick. We Westerners have gradually increased our intake of violence and sex over the years. Eastern Europeans, however, zoomed overnight from a culture of 1939 to 1990. People didn't have a framework to handle it.

Films were shown in their original language, with subtitles in Romanian. Curse words were never translated, so cop movies only had a fraction of their dialogue printed on the screen.

My landlords, the Vucescus, walked in. Dressed in their Sunday best, they had just been out for a stroll through Central Park, along with most of the town. Domnul Vucescu emptied his pockets onto the table by the front door, as though he still lived there.

I served them coffee, and we sat around the kitchen table to talk. The government had just raised the tax for rental property. They would need to pay the state 100% of what I paid them in rent. They asked me to sign a paper stating that I was their cousin. If we were family, they would not be taxed.

"We love you like family," Doamna Vucescu said.

As a team, we had talked through this potential scenario and decided what we should do. I told them that I couldn't lie, but I also didn't want them to pay such a ridiculous penalty. I offered to pay the tax for them. After all, my rent only cost $200. I could handle $400 for housing.

"But you don't understand," Doamna Vucescu said. "The money will go to the State. The State is corrupt. We don't want you to pay them."

"I have to pay," I said. "I don't feel right about saying something that is not true, although I understand why you asked me to. It's a small price for me to pay to be able to live in this beautiful country as a foreigner. I know that God blesses us when we do what is right, especially when it comes as a sacrifice. I love God, and I want to please Him in every area of my life. That is why I must do this."

"*Scumpa!* My precious girl," Domnul Vucescu said. "I have never known anyone like you. There must be something to this relationship with God after all."

The Vucescus stayed to fix a few things around the apartment with some tin foil, twine, and clothespins. Romanians never replaced anything they could possibly repair. They saved it all, even stitching together runners in nylons.

When they prepared to leave, Domnul Vucescu noticed that the table by the door only held keys. The coins were missing.

"Oh, she has done it again. You little thief." He laughed and wagged his forefinger at LaToya.

My cat was a kleptomaniac. She claimed any loose object as her own and buried it under my living room rug, exactly dead-center. I rolled back the carpet, and there were the coins.

Thankfully, Domnul Vucescu used to be a veterinarian. He thought LaToya was the cleverest cat in the world.

Soon it would be Christmas, my first Christmas spent in Romania and not Switzerland or Germany. Decorations were still not sold, but I did spot some hand-made ones. One of the kiosks downtown, which sold newspapers and cigarettes, sported a skinny tree on top. We called it the Charlie Brown tree. The owner had cut out stars to decorate it. It looked very festive—that is, until I got closer. Then I discovered that the stars had been cut from cigarette cartons.

Suzy, Kelly, and I scoured the city for gifts for our families. Despite the slim selection, we found some carved wooden pieces and handcrafted lace just in time. Rob and Paul were leaving for good before Christmas, and they offered to mail our gifts in the States.

We passed a small shop with plates in the window. The dishes had photo transfer faces of people on them. Suzy knew my brother and his family, and we decided it would be a truly unique gift for them to have a plate with our faces on it.

We hurried to my flat to get a photo of the two of us together, returning to the store before it closed. I asked if they could make a plate with our picture. The shopkeeper looked puzzled, but agreed to fill the order.

A few days later, I went to pick it up with Ildiko, one of my students.

"Terena," she whispered to me. "These plates are meant to be put on a grave. The picture is to be of the dead person."

No wonder I baffled the shopkeeper. He had probably never before encountered two living women who wanted to be buried together.

Suzy and me with our funeral plate.

I lived at the bottom of two hills, on the banks of the river. A dorm complex sat on top of each hill. I got a lot of exercise climbing to the dorms, often returning home well after midnight when the buses had quit for the day.

After one of our weekly fellowship meetings, all of the girls in my Bible study group tromped downhill for our final time together at my flat before the holiday. We walked arm-in-arm down an empty but slick street. A blanket of snow covered the city. Ramona took up one end of the chain and Zsuzsa had the other. In between were the Hungarians, Ildiko and Emese, the Romanians, Liana and Cătalina, and Suzy, Kelly, and me.

As we walked along, chattering, Ramona suddenly lost her footing. She fell with a thud on the icy road. Still holding on, the rest of us tumbled like dominoes. Soon there were nine of us girls sliding down the streets of Cluj. We made a rather long luge sled. When we reached the bottom of the hill, we tumbled into a pile, laughing.

"That was fun!" several said.

"Shall we go again?" Ramona asked.

David and Susan invited me to spend the night on Christmas Eve. After a hearty supper, we bundled up their newborn, Kathryn, and trudged through the silent city dusted with snow, headed for a beautiful service of traditional Romanian *colinde,* carols sung without instruments. The pastor read the story from Luke, but no other words were spoken.

Earlier, David and Susan had asked me about my family's traditions. I told them that we opened one gift on Christmas Eve, and it was always a nightgown or slippers to wear the next morning around the tree. Before we retired, they gave me a box to open. Inside sat wooly slippers and a flannel nightgown.

The smells of home—cinnamon rolls baking and freshly cut pine boughs—gently woke me on Christmas morning. I was with family. I didn't need to leave Romania to experience Christmas and family.

What About You?

- What makes you feel as though you're with family?

- If you were to establish a ministry, what foundations would you choose?

- Think of the ways you are already involved in service. How can you develop it more with prayer and logic-defying love?

Chapter 8

YOU CAN'T GET THERE FROM HERE

*"Do not fear, for I am with you; do not anxiously look
about you, for I am your God.
I will strengthen you, surely I will help you,
surely I will uphold you with My righteous right hand."*

—Isaiah 41:10

May 1994, Cluj-Napoca, Romania

I RUMMAGED AROUND the *piaţa* for John and Ann's wedding gift. I only had a few hours before my flight to Bucharest for staff meetings and Ann's bridal shower. David and Susan had already left by car. Once I bought the present, my to-do list would be nearly complete.

In a matter of days, I would return to the States for the summer. A family in my church had offered to take care of LaToya until I returned. That very morning, I gave them my cat to take to their grandmother's house in a village nearby. I hoped LaToya would like it there, but I had a sinking feeling that I might never see her again.

I browsed the shelves of ceramics. Every region in Europe had a unique pottery pattern. In Transylvania, the blue and white swirl pattern was handmade in an ethnic Hungarian hamlet called Korond, and sold in our market. I picked out the largest vase and headed home.

As I left the crowded *piața*, I sensed that someone followed me too closely. It felt uncomfortable. I crossed the river, and the person still trailed me.

"Where is the Hotel Napoca?" my shadow asked, as he stood facing the Hotel Napoca.

"There," I pointed, saying nothing more.

I had to think quickly. I didn't want him to know where I lived, so I ducked into the apartment building next to mine. He didn't follow me in. I waited in the shadows under the stairs for what seemed like five minutes. My heart's pounding was the only noise I heard.

I peeked out the doorway, did not see him, and dashed to my building, sprinting up my steps. Once I closed and locked my door, I could breathe again. I had fooled him.

I put the last items in my carry-on, and then settled down to read. My doorbell rang, and I jumped. When I looked through the peephole, I saw the guy who had followed me from the *piața*. I didn't answer, but I knew that he had heard me come to the door. He persisted a while, then finally left.

Fifteen minutes later, the telephone rang. Thinking it might be Ann in Bucharest, I answered.

"I am Alexandru. I want to see you," a man's voice said over the line.

I recognized his voice. "How did you get my number?" I asked.

"I heard you give it at the *poșta*."

I hadn't been to the post office since last week. He had been following me for days.

"I do not want to talk to you. Do not ever call me or come by again." I slammed the phone on the receiver.

The phone rang five more times before he gave up.

A few minutes later, I heard a scratching noise on my door. Alexandru had come back. "I want you," he whispered. I ignored him.

I was frightened. I prayed for God's protection and begged Him for wisdom.

I tried to call all the missionary men I knew to take me to the airport. No one was home. I called my regular taxi company. One of the drivers attended my church, and I asked for him by name. I needed a driver who would make me feel safe.

My taxi would be in front of the building in 10 minutes. I considered asking the taxi dispatcher to have the driver come up to my door. The dispatcher would probably think the worst, assuming all foreign women to be loose. I decided not to ask, because I didn't want his reputation, as a moral Christian, to be sullied. But I needed help.

I had to get past this potentially dangerous man. I grabbed the knives in my kitchen. *He'll probably be able to turn these against me, and I'll be the one who gets stabbed.* I put the knives back.

Then it came to me. I slid my right arm into John and Ann's vase. It went up to my shoulder. *If he's still there, I'll crack him over the head with this.* After all, the vase would be easy to replace.

I looked through the peephole and didn't see anyone. I quickly prayed again. Pulling my arm tightly into the vase and picking up my bag with my free hand, I cautiously opened the door. Nothing. I shot down the steps and onto the street. My taxi sat waiting for me. I was safe.

When I returned from Bucharest a few days later, David met me at the airport and drove me to their flat for dinner. When he took me home, he walked through my apartment first to check.

We made a plan to go to the police station in the morning, but for now, everything seemed in place.

In the middle of the night, my phone rang. It was Alexandru. I hung up.

Early that morning, the doorbell rang. The stalker had returned. I crept to the phone, situated right next to the door, and dialed David and Susan's number. David and I had planned a code.

"Now," I whispered.

Alexandru heard me and took off. I parted the lace curtain and watched him cross the bridge. He turned to stare at me, making a telephone motion with his hand at his ear. I felt a chill. He plopped on the park bench directly opposite my flat. I shivered, wondering how many months he had watched me from that vantage point, relieved my bedroom faced the other side.

When David arrived, 10 minutes later, I took him to the window so he could see my stalker. Alexandru was slight, with the same brown coat that he wore the other day. David sprinted to the park, but Alexandru had vanished.

As David chased him, Alexandru telephoned again. "I only want to get to know you. I love you," he said.

"Leave me alone." I slammed down the phone. I was shaking.

David drove me to the police station to file a report. We were escorted into the chief's office. I gave him all the details. He gave me his personal hot line number to call if Alexandru harassed me again, promising to end this nightmare. He also told me that once someone provides a street address, the telephone company gives the listing. Alexandru knew my address when he came to my door. It would have been easy to find the phone number.

Two more days remained before furlough. Students stayed with me in my apartment both nights so I would not be alone. Alexandru did not call again.

Summer 1994, Seaford, Delaware

I had not been in the States, or driven a car, for two and a half years. My mother had come to visit me once in Bucharest, in the middle of that time. When Delta Airlines started flying to Bucharest with an introductory offer, my mom and all my teammates' moms came to experience their children's new lives. Their visits breathed new life into us.

My niece, Lisa, was two and a half years old when we met for the first time. The whole family descended at my parents' house near the beach in Delaware. I had missed knowing Lisa as a baby. Her brothers had changed so much, too. Not being present for the kids' development had been one of the largest costs for me to count. It still hurt to see what I had given up.

I enjoyed my time with family and friends, visiting ministry partners, speaking in churches, stocking up on things to take back. Once again, the financial support I needed took no effort on my part. I simply wrote a letter, and people responded immediately.

Much too quickly, the summer passed, and I had to leave. The past year in Cluj had been my favorite year of ministry ever. Life would be different now. Suzy and Kelly left for good a month before I did. I could not imagine Cluj without them. My only consolation was knowing I'd always see Suzy in the States, because she lived near my brother in Arizona. Melynda, an American, and Florin, a Romanian, were coming from Bucharest to join our team.

I received a letter in the States saying that LaToya had run away from her temporary home in the village. I grieved the loss of my furry companion. I loved walking up the stairs to my flat and hearing her happy meow, knowing I had been missed. She had been God's gift to me through some difficult times, coming to me just after the police raid in Bucharest. Now she would not be there to welcome me home.

September 1994, Budapest, Hungary

Melynda met me at the airport in Budapest. After a day there, we boarded the train for the eight-hour trip home to Cluj. Whether I traveled by train, plane, or Dacia, something always seemed to go wrong. My teammates said that I attracted adventure.

"Melynda, I need to warn you," I said, once we settled into our seats. "If you hang around me, things will happen."

"What kind of things?"

"Well, let me tell you. When I left for furlough, I woke up in the middle of the night to see a Frenchman in my compartment, hovering over me with a rolled-up newspaper. He said he was trying to shoo away a rat scurrying across the floor. I didn't sleep anymore that trip."

I told her that our team often made this journey on substandard trains to stock up on supplies. The bathrooms on board were so deplorable that Suzy, Kelly, and I would purposely dehydrate ourselves, not drinking anything for hours before the trip so we wouldn't need to use them. As soon as we arrived in Budapest, we raced to the McDonald's in the train station to guzzle some liquid and, of course, eat cheeseburgers.

"Then there was the time I went to Budapest to meet David and Susan and baby Kathryn. They were bringing Katy home from Germany, and I helped them carry her baby things. Our friend, Jerry, met us at the Cluj station. David helped Susan and the baby off the train, and I handed the bags through the window to Jerry. The train only stopped for five minutes, so we had to be quick. As I tried to climb down, two gypsy men tied the door handle closed with ropes, trapping me with them in the hallway at the end of the car. One of them started to grab for me. I knew I had to get out of there fast, so I prayed and asked God to please help me. You know, I'm not very strong. But I pushed both of those men out of the way and pulled the ropes off the door, just as the train began to move. I have no explanation for that, other than God giving me a dose of His strength."

I also described to Melynda the time I returned by myself with bags full of diet coke and cat food. "The train took a detour and ended up in a village in Hungary which I had never heard of, and couldn't even begin to pronounce. I didn't know how to get back on the right track, but I knew the Hungarian words for help—*segitség*—and Cluj—*Kolozsvár*. So, I stood on the platform and called out to the group, '*Segitség! Kolozsvár?*' A man came forward, showed me a map, and pointed out the train I needed to take. Then he said, 'Sex, please? Hotel?' I said, 'No, thank you,' and walked away from him. I guess I didn't need to say thank you."

The man in our compartment listened attentively to my stories. I had assumed he didn't speak English.

"You are a very brave woman," he said. "May I ask what you do in Cluj?"

I explained our ministry to college students. He was fascinated.

"This is a very good work. You are filling a huge need. I will do whatever I can to see your work accomplished," he said.

He went on to identify himself as the Rector of Education at Babeş-Bolyai University in Cluj. Melynda and I were seated with the most influential person we could have met. We copied down his information and promised to bring David along next week to meet further. Our train friend proved to be an open door for our work over the years, moving up to become the Minister of Education for the entire country.

This time the train adventure was not a tragedy.

Immediately when I returned, I searched the entire flat but didn't find any signs of Alexandru. For days, I looked over my shoulder everywhere I went. He seemed to have disappeared. Life slowly started to become normal again, as normal as it could be with the absence of Suzy, Kelly, and LaToya the cat.

We jumped headfirst into a busy year of ministry. One day the team met in my flat to do some planning. The phone rang. It was Alexandru. I had almost forgotten about my stalker.

David grabbed the phone and yelled at him. He told him the police were after him.

I called the hot line number the police chief gave me. I pictured him answering a red phone, like the ones waiting for Krushchev and Kennedy during the Cold War.

Alexandru called and knocked at my door a few more times. Each time I called the police chief's number. After several weeks, the police came by with a message. They had nabbed my stalker. Maybe now I could begin to let down my guard.

Three girls had risen to the top of my discipleship group. They had caught the vision and started multiplying their lives spiritually into other students' lives. Melynda and these students each led Bible studies of their own, with the goal of teaching faithful people who would be able to teach others.

Cute and a bit spacey, Ramona had a great sense of humor and an ability to laugh at herself. She stood out from the typical brunette Romanians with her strawberry blonde hair. She would often show up on the wrong night or at the wrong place. Ramona had a gift for attracting people. We watched her shine in front of the group, performing in skits or making announcements.

Gentle Ildiko was the compassionate and merciful one, always thinking of others. Ildi had a knack for making people feel welcomed and cared about, as though no one else existed for her at that moment. She always sat with someone new at the meetings. She excelled at helping behind the scenes.

Zsuzsa had the leadership skills and unwavering commitment. She told me that since she had grown up under Communism, as part of the Hungarian minority in Romania, she felt that God had uniquely prepared her to go somewhere difficult to reach oppressed people for Christ. With her straight black hair, Asia seemed a natural fit. "If it's not me, then who will it be?" she asked.

Students at a party in Cluj.

We filled a bus with our students and headed to a retreat where we would meet the gang from Bucharest. Our destination, Cozia, sat halfway between the two cities. After we started to climb the winding mountain roads, our driver stopped to let about 10 students out to throw up.

The toxic bus fumes didn't help matters. Many of these students had never been on a road trip before. They had only ridden on public transportation in cities.

Melynda and I had each brought Dramamine from the States for travel sickness. We walked down the aisle and doled it out to everyone who felt queasy. Soon they were fast asleep.

During our five-hour ride, we sang songs of worship and played games. One game involved two sweaters. We asked for volunteers, and Dan quickly offered his pullover. Dan was a brilliant medical student with a heart of gold. Fully sold out to

131

Christ, he dreamed of practicing medicine for people who had no other options and probably couldn't pay. I had known Dan for two years now, and I had only seen him wear one sweater, a blue-gray pullover.

The game involved passing a sweater from person to person on each side of the bus. One person would put it on right-side out, then the person in the next row would take it off and slip it on themselves wrong-side out. The goal was to pass your sweater quickly so that it made it to the back before the sweater on the other side did. I hoped Dan's only sweater would not get stretched out of shape.

On the return trip, Melynda and I passed out the Dramamine before the bus started to roll.

Cluj and Bucharest students at a retreat in Cozia, Romania.

The Romanian car model, the Dacia, was copied after the French Renault. I knew people who truly believed the propaganda that the Dacia was the best car in the world. In the Soviet Bloc, nearly every country manufactured its own car. Each person who drove (a small percentage of the population) had the same car as everyone else.

Czechoslovakia had the Skoda, Yugoslavia the Yugo, and Russia the Lada. The common denominator was that none of them worked very well. Romanians even made fun of the East German Trabant, considered the bottom of the barrel.

In the beginning of my life in Romania, people seemed to be content with the little they had. They didn't know what they lacked. Their technology had stopped when World War II broke out. The home appliances resembled the ones I saw in old Katharine Hepburn and Cary Grant movies, 50 years behind the times.

I wanted to shelter them from the real world. I didn't want them to ever find out. As the West began to infiltrate, Romanians started observing what the rest of the world had that they did not. Discontent dawned.

They had artificial glimpses of life in the West through American films, television shows such as *Dallas*, and German appliances displayed in store windows. There were no McDonald's or Western hotels yet, sure signs of financial growth in developing countries.

Under Communism, Romanians had no national or personal debt. Nothing was imported. Only food grown in Romania, in season, was sold. That explained the scarcity of food in the winter, and the lack of tropical fruits. People only bought what they could pay for in cash. They didn't realize that one of the reasons the Westerners in the films had so many belongings is that they bought what they could not afford, sinking into debt.

In Cluj, I found like-minded friends outside of my team and students. I met Mioara, a Philosophy professor, after one

133

of our events on campus. We would sit and talk for hours, often about novels that had touched our souls. We were the same age and enjoyed the same things. We both described our ideal day as curling up on a sofa with an afghan, reading a good book, and drinking hot chocolate. We dreamed aloud about the places we wanted to see before we die, still an impossible vision for my new friend.

Mioara told me that books had been her only escape. The Communists had tried to squelch individualism, but when she got lost in a story, she forgot about reality. Most Romanians I knew were voracious readers and had stacks of paperback books. Besides British authors like Dickens and Austen, Mark Twain and Louisa May Alcott had also been translated.

The first time I visited Mioara in her flat, she showed me her contraband typewriter, illegal during the former regime. She also showed me her stuffed dog, Laika, in her bookcase. Every Soviet Bloc child had adored the first dog in space. Laika, a mutt from Moscow, had paved the way for cosmonaut Yuri Gagarin to orbit in 1961. Those were heady days for the Soviets, winning the space race against the Americans. As a small child, Mioara said she cried inconsolably when Laika died aboard Sputnik II.

Rodica and I met in church. We were also about the same age. Rodica asked if we could get together each week as prayer partners. The first time we were to meet, I said in Romanian, "I go to you." I waited at Rodica's for a while, but she had gone to my flat. She claimed I said, "You go to me." The dative form of the verb had risen up and bitten me.

I loved doing ministry with college students, but I didn't enjoy being in the dorms so late every evening. I wondered how long I could keep up this pace. At 38, I longed for a schedule that ended at a more normal time of day. I wanted to step back and help equip younger staff members to be the ones to work with the students.

When asked to assume a traveling and shepherding position with Campus Crusade staff throughout Eastern Europe, I knew this must be the role for me. The only hitch was that it involved moving to Budapest, Hungary. I loved living in Cluj, but I sensed God nudging me to go.

After emotional farewells with the team and students I adored, I had to start the logistical process of moving. The good-byes were made a little easier knowing that I would travel to Romania frequently in my new position. In fact, I had already planned my first trip back for the fall.

Moving across an unfriendly border was fraught with difficulty and bureaucracy. I met with the Chief of Customs to obtain permission to move my possessions out of Romania. He gave me a long list of documents I needed to bring to him. I brought them the next day. He seemed surprised that I returned so quickly, and he demanded even more information.

This time, it proved to be a little harder to round up. As I bounced between one office and another, I kept hearing, "You can't move there from here. You can't move to Hungary from Romania." Someone even suggested I move to the United States first, and then from there to Hungary.

I took the train to Budapest to find an apartment and open a bank account, prerequisites to applying for a residence permit. I also had my future office write me a letter of invitation to live there. I had to start the residence permit process in Hungary before I could get a visa in Romania, which was necessary before I could actually obtain the residence permit. It felt like a vicious game of which came first, the residence permit or the visa.

Once I had those papers, I flew to Bucharest, Romania. Within an hour, I received a new passport at the American Consulate and an official letter, stating that I had been an upstanding resident of Romania and asking favor to let me depart with my belongings. Amazingly, it only took 15 minutes to get my visa at the Hungarian Consulate in Bucharest. Things were looking up.

I had all the papers the Chief had requested. When I entered the Chief's office in Cluj, I knew that he held the power to release me. I put on my most deferential voice. "*Bună dimineața.* Good morning, Domnul Chief of All Chiefs, Sir. It is so good of you to see me."

I handed him the papers, and he perused them silently for several minutes, looking up a few times to study me.

"You can leave, but you cannot take any of your belongings," he said.

"But they are my personal belongings. Am I supposed to leave photographs of my family by the side of the road?" I said, sarcasm dripping from my voice.

"You still need a receipt proving that you exchanged more American money in Romania than the total value of your goods."

I didn't know how I could get those papers. My eyes filled with tears. It seemed as though I stood in the presence of the Wizard of Oz. The wizard had asked Dorothy and her friends to bring back the witch's broom, assuming that would never happen, because they needed to kill the witch to get it. This Chief had given me assignments he never expected me to fulfill. Against all odds, I kept returning with the impossible items, but each time it turned out to be an empty goal.

"Domnișoara Richardson, I want to help you. I want you to succeed," he said, looking me in the eyes. I began to believe he might mean it.

I went home to my flat filled with boxes and had a good cry. I turned to the Lord for comfort. Opening my Bible to I Kings 17, I read about God taking care of Elijah's needs during the drought through unlikely sources, some ravens and a widow. "Father, I will wait on You to provide what I need. My hope is in You."

That day I talked to the Syrian men who ran the exchange place. Their dark skin reminded me of ravens. They never gave receipts, laughing instead whenever I requested them. I explained my predicament to them.

"Is there anyway you can look through your books to total up the amount of money I've exchanged here these last two years?" I asked. "I realize this is a big job. I am sorry, but I have nowhere else to turn."

"Come back tomorrow, and we'll see what we can do," one of them said.

The next day, they presented me with a receipt. "We know you come here regularly. We are also foreigners, and we also have to live by these crazy rules. The boss wrote you a receipt which gives his estimate of the total amount you have exchanged."

It was more than I needed. They were my ravens.

Everything seemed to be in order now. I listed all my belongings with a dollar value next to each item and loaded it all into a friend's truck. The sofa I bought from friends who had left had been impounded by their landlord, so I had to pick that up from the police station where it had served its time. Radu and Lucian, two men I barely knew from my church, drove the truck with me in it to Customs. Before I could leave, the Chief needed to seal the truck.

"Good, good," the Chief said as he looked at my receipt. "Everything on your list can be taken out of the country except for your paintings. There is a new directive about art leaving Romania. You need documents showing that your shipment of artwork entered the country legally."

I felt sick. If I couldn't prove the legality of my paintings, made by me and signed by me, they would become the property of Romania. They would have to remain in Romania.

When my boxes of personal household items and artwork had arrived in 1992, I never obtained any paperwork when I picked them up from Customs in the airport. I had asked for a receipt and had been told it wasn't necessary. I had the paperwork from the States, proving they were shipped. That is where the paper trail ended.

I explained this to the Chief, and he placed a telephone call to Customs in the Bucharest airport.

I remembered I had gone alone that day. All the men on my team were busy. Susan had prayed specifically for my protection. She asked God to send a woman to help me and keep me safe from the lewd men. God had provided a woman, a sweet elderly one. She had to be too old now to still be working.

"*Da, da.* Yes, yes. January 1992," the Chief spoke into the phone. "A pretty American girl. You remember her? *Extraordinar. Da, da.* I need a faxed copy with the shipping number. *Imediat.*"

He turned to me. "It is an old woman. She remembers you." He seemed incredulous.

This precious lady is my unlikely widow. More than three years later, she is still working.

Within 30 minutes, the fax machine hummed. The document came through. The Chief signed and stamped all of my papers. He shook his head, smiled, and said, "*Gata!* Ready!" We walked outside, and he sealed the truck, not to be opened by anyone except for Hungarian Customs officers.

That old woman in Bucharest had been the specific answer to prayer on my behalf once before. Today she filled that role again. Her presence reminded me that God cared about me, about every detail. He could move mountains to enable me to do what He called me to do. He could provide for me through ravens and a widow.

I prayed that just as God overflowed the widow's supply who took care of Elijah, this dear woman's life would never run dry of blessings all the rest of her days.

Now I could leave Romania. The next hurdle would be entering Hungary.

What About You?

- Think of times you have felt afraid. How has God protected you in scary situations?

- Has there ever been a situation that appeared impossible—as though you can't get there from here? How did you experience His provision?

- Who have been some of the unlikely sources, ravens or widows, through which He has provided for you?

Chapter 9

HUNGARIAN
RHAPSODY

Faithful is He who calls you, and He also will bring it to pass.

—1 Thessalonians 5:24

July 1995, Budapest, Hungary

RADU, LUCIAN, AND I left Cluj the afternoon of July 3rd with all the contents of my moving truck sealed up tightly. We bounced along rutted mountain roads, and I wondered how many of my plates and glasses would be sacrificed. The Romanian guards nodded and waved us through the border. The Customs seal did the trick.

It was a different story at the Hungarian side. The seal, the Romanian documents, even the U.S. Consulate letter, none of it mattered. The officials rudely scoffed at us, disparaging my two Romanian drivers. Well after dark, they finally let us proceed.

We arrived in the middle of the night. I hated knocking on my colleague's door so late, but it would not look proper to my neighbors if two men stayed at my apartment.

Once again, I celebrated the Fourth of July by moving. It was exactly two years to the day since I had moved to Cluj.

Radu and Lucian remained in Budapest two days until Hungarian Customs came to unseal the truck. The translator from my new office, Gábor, arrived to wait with us. He stood in the kitchen.

"Gábor, please, come sit in the living room and have some coffee," I said.

"No, those Romanians are there." He pointed to Radu and Lucian. "I will stay in this room."

I spent the day walking between the two rooms, refilling coffees and offering lunch, because Gábor's pride didn't let him associate with Romanians. I felt the sting of his prejudice personally.

The Customs man arrived the second day and said that I still needed a bond paper before I could open my boxes.

"Can we at least unload the truck so the drivers can return to Kolozsvár?" I asked.

"*Igen.* Yes," he said. "However, you must promise not to open the boxes until I return to authorize them."

We moved everything inside, and Radu and Lucian took their leave. These two men, whom I hardly knew, had been with me every day for four days. They had protected me like big brothers and given up quite a bit of income by missing work. I slipped a wad of bills inside a letter thanking them and their wives, and put it inside their truck.

When everyone had left, I walked through my new apartment and prayed room by room, thanking God for my beautiful flat and asking Him to make it be a haven to all who would enter. My new home had two bedrooms, a living room, and a kitchen—the same as my flats in Bucharest and Cluj. The layout looked much more interesting and spacious. The four rooms were stacked on top of each other, one room per floor. I felt spoiled to live alone in a four-floor apartment, but I trusted that many others would enjoy this refuge with me.

During the next few days, I made my way from one office to another, waiting for final clearance to become a legal resident of Hungary. In every line, I saw the same reaction when Hungarians typed my birth date. They crossed themselves. The day of my birth was the blackest day in their recent history. In late October 1956, Hungarians tasted freedom for 12 days before Soviet tanks rolled in to quash that, the day I was born. I saw pictures of demolished bridges and shells of buildings with a backdrop of smoke. Many courageous people lost their lives. The brightest and best of a whole generation fled the country for Austria, most migrating to America, often ending up in the film industry.

The owner of my apartment lived in Paris. I paid the rent and communicated any problems to his brother, László, who lived in Budapest. László spoke perfect English. He came over to whitewash the walls and help me move furniture from room to room. His brother had left behind beautiful antique settees and armoires that I could use. As we covered all the furniture snugly with plastic, I told him about the effect my birthday had on people.

"We are the same age, you and I," he said, setting down the machine in the center of the living room. "I was born at home one month after you. The hospitals in Budapest were all destroyed. It was a very difficult time for my mother."

László flipped a switch, and the machine began to spray each wall and everything else in its path, covered or not, including the windows and floors. I knew about whitewashed walls from Romania. I had scrubbed the chalky film off my clothes countless times, smeared on by leaning against walls. I longed for a can of Sherwin-Williams and some color.

"We waited for the Americans to come and save us," László said. "We waited you, but you didn't come." I had heard those words before.

László had given me permission to box up any of his brother's belongings that I didn't want and store them in the attic. The floor-to-ceiling bookcases in the top bedroom burst with Hungarian books that I couldn't read. As I loaded the volumes from the top shelf into boxes, I lost my balance, and a heavy textbook tumbled out of my arms. Eleven crisp $100 bills, American money, slid onto the floor.

My move had been costly. *God, could this be Your gift to me?* Tempted to pocket the money, I stopped myself. This money belonged to someone, not to me, and I needed to try to find out whom. I called one of my teammates to tell her what I planned to do, so she would keep me accountable. The next morning, I took the tram to my bank and deposited the stash into my dollar account, to keep it safe while I looked for the owner.

I tracked down telephone numbers for the Americans who rented the flat before me. They had not left any money behind. My landlord said his brother, an absent-minded scientist, had been in the habit of hiding hard currency in his home. The brother didn't remember leaving $1,100, but it followed that a preoccupied person might not recall details from years before. It made sense that the money belonged to him. After all, the flat and the book were his.

I returned the money to László to send to his brother. They were both amazed that I would do that and promised not to forget.

I had most of the summer to settle in to my new life. My new job would not begin until September, when my teammates were due to return from summer furloughs. I had fallen in love with Budapest when I lived in Cluj and visited this gem on the Danube. That summer, we became better acquainted. I leisurely rode buses and trams, exploring every corner, ending up sipping coffee at the Gerbeaud while listening to string quartets or strolling along the banks of the river, serenaded by violinists.

I discovered that three cities combined to form Budapest in the late 1800s: the hilly left bank of the Danube called Buda, the flat side called Pest, and the northern part called Óbuda. Budapest had 22 districts, radiating out from the center. The stunning first district had gas lamps and cobblestone streets, Matthias Church, and the Royal Palace. The less prestigious districts had higher numbers and were situated on the outer rim.

I lived in District XXII, the very last and lowliest district. The massive statues of Lenin and Marx, which I had seen on their pedestals downtown five years before, had recently been rounded up and moved near my flat. Rather than destroy the statues, they were preserved for history in an inconspicuous location.

Many mission groups had their Eastern European head-quarters in Budapest, and these groups consisted of families and single women, with single men lacking. I got to know most of the single women that summer. We would go out to lunch together, ordering *paprikás csirke* (chicken with paprika, Hungary's favorite spice) or *gulyásleves* (goulash soup cooked in a black iron cauldron hanging from a tripod over an open fire).

I discovered that Hungarians loved film. Budapest had many brand-new movie theaters with cafés in the lobby, stadium seating, and cushy chairs. The American films, subtitled in Hungarian, were more recent than the ones in Romania. The earliest film started about 9:00 each morning and they continued until midnight. When my new friends and I went to a film on a weekday afternoon, only a few other people were inside. Movie tickets had assigned seat numbers. With nine empty rows behind us and 10 in front of us, we were assigned to the same row as the other patrons, with no vacant seats in-between. If we left a seat free, or sat in the row behind, the other moviegoers would take it upon themselves to insist we move. This happened more than once. This habit, policing others to follow the rules so negative repercussions wouldn't fall on oneself, died hard in this part of the world.

That summer, I joined an intensive class in the Magyar language. Hungarian is one of the most difficult languages for native English speakers to learn, so I wanted to get a jump-start. I learned the words *"Hogy van"* for "How are you" and the textbook answer *"Köszönöm, jól"* for "Thank you, I am well." My teacher said we would never hear that answer in Hungary; rather, *"nem jól,"* followed by a diatribe of all the reasons the person was not well. She cautioned us not to ask unless we had at least 15 minutes free.

I read up on the history of Hungary, or Magyarország. The Magyars originally migrated from Mongolia. Some settled in Hungary in 896 A.D. and others went north to Finland. They were barbarian warriors who lived in tents called yurts and did battle with Attila and the Huns. Vestiges of various empires remained—Roman, Ottoman, and Austro-Hungarian. In fact, Hungary claims to have saved Western Europe by stopping the Ottoman Turks.

An Italian missionary named Gellért tried to win the savages to Christianity but didn't receive a warm welcome. The people stuffed him in a barrel, drove swords into it, and then rolled it down the hill into the Danube to make sure he had died. King Istvan (Stephen) is credited with converting his people to Christianity a few years later, about 1000 A.D., by saying, "Convert, or die!" Thankfully, strategies had changed. Both men were later sainted. The hill where Gellért met his death bears his name. Istvan's mummified relic, his Holy Right Hand, is paraded through the streets of Budapest every year on August 20 (Saint Stephen's Day).

Hungarians did not hold back one bit during their millennium celebrations in 1896, attempting to rival Paris. Massive and ornate buildings in Pest were constructed for the world exhibition. The wide tree-lined Andrássy Boulevard showcased the elegant Opera House, Heroes' Square, and City Park, with the first subway in continental Europe still running below.

Many pureblooded Hungarians had straight dark hair, proving their Mongolian heritage, but most had melted in the pot with blonde Austrians and Germans nearby. Melancholia seemed to especially afflict this people group. Curiously, Finns, who shared the same origin, had the highest suicide rate in the world, and Hungarians had the second highest.

Melancholia was so pervasive that many Hungarians considered it their major national characteristic. Others took pride in their uniqueness. After all, they were Asians who became Europeans, with a language like none other. The numbers of these distinctive people were small. Only 10 million lived within the country's borders, while another 10 million Hungarians lived outside, mostly in the U.S.—a fact which magnified their despondency.

I loved everything about Hungary, except the prejudice I sensed toward my beloved Romanians. This tension, more emotionally charged here than in Cluj, stemmed from the fact that Transylvania now belonged to Romania. I didn't get it. Romanians didn't take the land from Hungary; the Allies parceled it out and re-drew national borders. It was the price for fighting on the wrong side in World War I. As an American who is oriented toward the future and not the past, I realized I didn't understand all the issues.

October–November 1995, Romania, Bulgaria, and Croatia

I traveled back to Romania for my first official trip as part of the area leadership team, keeping my promise to return soon. My reunion was a joyful one, helped by the food and books I carted along to distribute to our teams in all three cities—Bucharest, Cluj, and our newest team in Iaşi. From there, I journeyed to

Bulgaria to meet with the team in Sofia. The first Bulgarian national, Velislava, had just joined our staff.

I felt weary but satisfied as I rode the Mini-Busz home from the Budapest airport. The snow made the city glisten. As soon as I walked inside my apartment, I turned up the thermostat and started to sort my mail. The heat didn't kick in, so I turned it up a notch and began unpacking. After several more minutes, I realized it wasn't working. I hurried next door to ask Agota if she knew what I should do.

"Miklos in apartment three is our handyman," she said. "I will call him for you."

My small building housed six flats. Agota explained to me that we were all family, and to please ask whenever I needed help with anything. The neighbors had known each other for years. They built the row house together, with substandard materials, during the Communist days, so things were bound to break. The neighbors were all professionals—an architect, an engineer, a dentist, and two professors. Most of them spoke English fluently, and many were believers.

Miklos arrived quickly and worked on my heat until midnight. I fell into bed, wrapped in my down comforter and wearing my warmest layers, exhausted.

A few days later, I boarded the eight-hour train for Zagreb, Croatia. As soon as we crossed the border, the white U.N. tanks, jeeps, and ambulances were visible along the tracks. That same week in November, peace accords were being worked out in Dayton, Ohio to end the three-and-a-half year Bosnian war. While at a prayer meeting with the staff team, four bombs detonated as armament testing. The noise shook me and made me feel the reality of war.

That night I met many of the students involved in the ministry and spoke at their meeting. Looking out at the fun-loving young people, more sophisticated than Romanians, I tried to imagine the hurts in their lives that Christ filled.

"Every Croat has experienced the pain of war," Biljena said. "We are a small country of just four million. We've all lost a friend or relative. I lost my entire village. After my family fled from Sisak, we returned to see that our house had been bombed. We were homeless. Christ is teaching me that He is all I need, and that it's possible to forgive."

Zrinka and I met for coffee the next day. As we left the café, Zrinka showed me a brick wall in the center of the city. Many bricks bore the name of an MIA or POW. Some had been painted black.

"What does the black mean?" I asked.

"Those are the people who have died. This was my brother's brick. It is black now."

"I am so sorry, Zrinka." I put my hand on her shoulder.

"Yes, it was a terrible loss. I did not think life was worth living after that. When I returned to university, some students told me that Jesus loved me. I needed to hear that. I had nowhere else to turn. I gave my life to Him at that time. Something good came out of my grief."

December 1995, Tirana, Albania

I was not prepared for what I saw in Albania. Like Romania, the chaotic airport didn't have any automated equipment, and taxi drivers hounded me like paparazzi. Nikki, who co-led the team, waited outside to hustle me into the vehicle.

"Taryn, meet Sneezy," she said, patting the dashboard. The ministry in Albania owned seven Land Rovers, named after the seven dwarfs, necessary to traverse this country with its impassable or nonexistent roads.

Round concrete bunkers dotted the roadside, detracting from the beauty of the mountains in the distance. I had read that there were over 600,000 bunkers—enough for every citizen of Albania to take refuge when the United States bombed them. The people had been brainwashed by their paranoid dictator, Enver Hoxha, and completely cut off from any news of the outside world. Communism had worked more effectively in Albania than any other country in the Soviet Bloc. Albanians truly believed an attack was imminent. They also bought the propaganda that they were the lighthouse of the world.

Shepherds herded their sheep down the rutted dirt roads of the capital city, as bikes and cars weaved wildly through traffic. One bike had two pigs tied upside down on the ends of the handlebars.

"No one here has driven longer than three years," Nikki said, and it showed. "They were not allowed to own cars or get driver's licenses under Communism."

As we turned onto a narrow road, I saw tiny houses with walls enclosing miniature courtyards, instead of the usual skyscraper block buildings. The abject poverty stood in sharp contrast to the palm trees and blue Adriatic Sea visible from the plane. Some of the walls bore red Communist stars and signs. Nikki translated. "This house helped hide Anti-Fascists."

I dropped my bags in the house where Nikki rented a room, and she called to let the others know I had arrived safely. Telephone lines didn't exist in Albania, so she picked up a ham radio, speaking to people called Foxtrot and Tango, calling herself November. The bathrooms stood outside in the courtyard. None of the homes had heat or hot water. The fact that Albania had a temperate climate saved them, although the constant rain all winter meant that they never got dry. Because of the climate, fruit and vegetables were available all year at the market.

It started to pour that day and didn't stop until after I left at the end of the week. The dirt roads quickly turned to mud. Walking to the weekly meeting that night meant fording several small rivers with my leaky boots.

Once inside, I entered an electric atmosphere, completely transformed. The joy of Christ radiated from 150 petite students in a way that thawed my chill. As Nikki introduced me, I drowned in hugs and kisses from people with no need for personal space. I decided that when I needed to feel affirmed, I would come to Tirana. Rather than kiss twice as Romanians do, affectionate Albanians kiss three times, sometimes more.

Just four years ago, in 1991, Albania was considered the first and only completely atheistic country, with a Muslim heritage before Communism wiped out religion. There were actually 12 known believers at that time, out of three million. In 1993, the first Stint team moved to Tirana to share the good news of Christ with people who had never heard His name. None of the students in this room had been believers for more than two years.

Nikki asked Brikena if she would tell me her story. Brikena shook her head.

Her answer surprised me, but I didn't want to intrude. Nikki whispered to me that Albanians shake their heads for "yes" and nod for "no."

Brikena had been raised knowing that she could never believe anything in print. While studying at the university, an American Stinter gave her a copy of a New Testament. She read it, curious to know about these fables. Brikena felt compelled by the character of Jesus. After she finished the fourth gospel, she decided those accounts of Jesus had to be true, because they were written by four different men who witnessed the same things. Brikena invited Jesus to take control of her life, joined our staff last year, and now trained five student leaders.

Mirjeta told me that her whole village gave their lives to Christ when a helicopter dropped down from the sky two summers before. The Americans on board were armed with a generator and a *Jesus* film in the Albanian language. After showing the film on bed sheets strung from trees, the guests stayed in the mountain village several days to talk more about Jesus. Mirjeta moved to

151

Tirana to attend the university and met up with that same group who had descended from above that day, the group with the lofty goal of taking the gospel to every single village in the country.

The female student leaders gathered to hear from me, at the home shared by the national staff women. I had barely started talking from my notes when the electricity went out, again. Lindita lit a candle for me to hold. I held my papers in my right hand and tried to steady the candle in my left as wax dripped from my hand onto my notes. It didn't matter. I ended up putting them aside and sharing my story from my heart. The girls cried, smothered me with more kisses, and enveloped me in their love.

Alma told the girls they could ask me questions. I kept forgetting whether to shake or nod my head, so when asked a question, I just rolled my head in a circle like a bobble head doll. They laughed and kissed me more.

When I arrived home to Budapest, this time my hot water pipes had burst. I called faithful Miklos to rescue me again.

By Christmas, I had traveled enough to know this new role fit me well. I also experienced the unglamorous side, the toll it took on me. I had set a personal goal of traveling to each of our countries every year, already having scheduled trips to Poland, Czech Republic, Slovakia, and Serbia for the spring. That meant being away from my home in Budapest half of each month and ministering to hundreds of staff.

My challenge was to make sure all the women staff throughout the area were shepherded. This worked fine in countries with 10 staff, where I could maintain regular individual contact. However, in countries with 100 staff, we had to set up a structure so that everyone had someone to care for them. On those trips, I met with the women in positions of countrywide leadership, each campus team leader, and team leaders for our other ministries (*Jesus* film, high school, young professionals, Family Life).

The conferences in Budapest were highlights for me. We'd often bring groups of staff to us for training, such as campus team leaders from each country or Stint teams arriving from the States. I loved those days when my home hummed with friends, arriving for a party or staying over the weekend after a conference.

Training conference for new campus leadership women throughout the area.

The trips were a spiritual high, an adventure, a chance to connect with my dear friends. I would return to Budapest, physically exhausted and utterly spent, to deal with the next disaster alone in my empty apartment. I began to dread coming home. I loved each person on my team individually, but as a whole, we weren't family like my other teams with Campus Crusade had been, both in the States and especially in Romania.

On this particular traveling team of 12 married couples and myself, we all took care of ourselves. The men I worked with returned home to reconnect with their families. No one offered to meet me at the airport or train station when I came back alone. I understood the impossible burden of welcoming me home every few weeks when they constantly traveled themselves, and

I tried not to take it personally. After all, their own wives didn't meet them either; we all took the Airport Mini-Busz. Still, I wished it was different.

Most of the time, I felt content being single. I knew I could never travel as I did if I had young children. I also knew God hadn't brought the right man along yet, and I'd rather be single than settle. I clung to His promises to provide all I need, to never withhold any good thing from me, and that I was complete in Him alone. Still, it bothered me if others seemed to think something was wrong with me while I tried my best to wait on God, trusting Him with my future.

It helped to plan ahead—before each trip—and set up a social time with a friend for shortly after my return. When I arrived home drained, I needed to rest by spending time alone reading and journaling, but if I had too much solitary time I would start to feel depressed. And I learned that it's hard to muster up the effort for a simple phone call when you have no emotional energy.

My intimacy with Christ grew as I learned to delight in Him alone as I never had before. He became my haven. Many times, when my loneliness felt more acute and I poured that out to Him, the phone would ring. "I was just thinking about you," my friend would say.

God filled the vacant spot I had expected my team to satisfy with a variety of people in Budapest. He faithfully provided the emotional support I needed to do what He called me to do. Sue, who served on the other Campus Crusade team in our city—the one overseeing the ministry in the country of Hungary, quickly became a kindred spirit friend. Sue and I could talk about anything, and usually did. We connected on a deep level, while other single women met many of my social needs.

"Taryn, I have to tell you something," Sue said one day. We had gone to explore Szentendre, a quaint neighboring village. "Your friendship is valuable to me, and I don't want anything to stand in the way. I love Hungarians, and when you criticize them, it hurts me."

I thanked her for caring enough to speak truth to me, and I asked her forgiveness. I explained that I didn't like the way Hungarians put down my Romanians, and I had let this become a barrier preventing me from fully embracing Hungary. I heeded her words and began to ask God to give me His love for the people among whom I now lived.

One of the people who helped me with this was my neighbor, Agota. She showed me the best of the Hungarian culture. I had long felt a connection to Hungary because of my birthday. In Cluj, I had come to know and love many wonderful ethnic Hungarians. Now God was answering my prayer and causing the bond already in place to grow stronger.

Agota had a heart for telling people about Jesus. She taught Bible stories and songs to a public kindergarten class each week, and she shared Christ with all of her teenage babysitters. Agota loved de-briefing with me after my trips, rejoicing in the changed lives and weeping over the difficult circumstances other believers faced. She knew my travel schedule, and she was the person who would know if my plane didn't land.

We had a fenced-in yard around our building and rotated the seasonal chores such as mowing grass, raking leaves, and shoveling snow. Her girls came out to "help" when I took my turn—by jumping in the pile of leaves or snow and shyly practicing their English words. Reka, Orsolya, and Margit were like stair-steps, with the oldest just six years old. Emese, the baby, was born the week before I moved in, so I always had a visual gauge as to how long I had lived in Budapest.

I learned to depend on the Holy Spirit in new ways as I traveled. The train or plane rides were great times to pray for each staff member by name: "Lord, You know what this person has cried out to You from the depths of their heart. I don't. I need Your Spirit to bring Your truth to my mind so I can say the words they need to hear. Empower me to be, to say, and to do what they need me to be, to say, and to do. Let me be Your arms to hug them."

Often I felt completely squeezed dry, with not one ounce left to dribble out. At those times I'd pray, "Father, I am so weary, I can't do this. But I know You can. I'm trusting You to give me the energy and enable me to do what You've called me to do. Fill me up so I will overflow. Please refresh me as You use me to refresh others." And He faithfully did. Every time.

June 1996, Budapest, Hungary

Each time I returned from a trip, my upper back muscles ached. I finally visited a physiotherapist named Kati, who had studied in the States. She worked on my trapezius muscle for months. I learned I could manage the pain by avoiding stress, sleeping well, and not carrying heavy things. That about summed up my traveling lifestyle. Besides daily exercises at home, she instructed me not to use my left arm at all for several weeks.

Bus trips to the *piac* (Hungarian *piaţa*) were especially challenging. Usually the bus was full on the return trip, so I had to stand, with my bags in my right hand or straddled between my feet. I couldn't use my left hand to hold on to the overhead loop. One day, I lost my balance as the bus careened around a sharp curve going uphill. My groceries fell onto the filthy floor. Eggs and oranges rolled everywhere, shot back and forth like a pinball machine. All but one egg broke. I got off the bus and trudged back to the *piac* to start again.

The time had come to look for a car, after not having one for six years. Brooke and Karen, my good friends in Zagreb, needed a mini-van before their fourth child came. They called me to see if I'd be interested in their Volkswagen station wagon. The price was more than fair.

"It's bright red, isn't it?" I asked, wishing for my favorite color. "Oh, I forgot, what's the name of the model?"

Brooke's answer sounded like "Passant." I'm sure I heard an "n" in there. I still spelled words the Romanian way, so to me the word was *Pìssant*. I quickly wrote my family and friends to tell them I had just made a deal to buy a Pissant. I didn't realize what I had said.

The Pissant lived up to its name. When I first began to notice the problems, I thought I was losing my mind. I would be certain that I had put the windows up, only to return to the car with them down. One morning, I found the windows down and a cat sleeping in the back seat. The car would not start. The battery had died.

It turned out that my car had an electrical short, which no mechanic seemed able to locate. The windows would go up and down with the engine off, usually in the middle of the night. Some mornings, snow or leaves filled my car. I began to refer to my Pissant as demon-possessed.

The car cost me more in mechanics' bills and frustration than the benefits I received. At the most, I only drove it a couple times a week, but I could never count on it. I found out that Budapest had more car theft than any other city in Europe. I began to pray it would be stolen so I could collect the insurance money. However, it had to be locked with the club on in order to collect, and I wanted to be above-board. When I would leave for a weeklong trip, I would drive my car to the most unsafe part of the city, secure the club, and lock it. My car was always there when I returned, windows down, covered in snow. No one else wanted it either.

I hadn't left my knack for attracting adventure behind in Romania. One night, as I sat on my sofa, I heard a loud pop, then a noise in the walls like aluminum foil being crinkled. The house went dark. Miklos rigged up a temporary solution for my electricity. The next night, the same crinkly noise woke me up.

I sat up in bed and watched a blue flame shoot out of the wall, missing my head by inches. Once again, the electricity went out, but this time a sickening odor, reminding me of incinerating chickens when I was a child, lingered for days. The inferior electrical wires had given out at last.

My regular bus had broken down, so all of the passengers packed into another one. I took a deep breath and squeezed in. *Someone is going to get pick-pocketed today.* I knew it couldn't be me. I had survived five years in Romania without being robbed. Besides, I always held onto my purse and wore the strap diagonally across my body.

When I stepped off the bus, I glanced at my purse. Someone had slit it with a knife. I reached inside. My wallet was not there.

As reality registered in my brain, the bus started to leave. A guy grinned at me through the window, shrugging with his palms up, as if to say, "Too bad, sucker."

I felt as though my feet were frozen in place, but somehow I forced them to move. I mentally listed the things I needed to do. Go to the American Consulate, file a report with the police, call home to cancel my credit cards. I put my emotions aside and went into task mode, accomplishing the first two items quickly in spite of unsympathetic, even callous people who waited on me.

Calling home presented a challenge. I had no money for a pay phone or ID to go to my bank to withdraw money. I decided to step inside an American hotel and see if they could help. I explained my story to the concierge at the Marriott. His nametag identified him as "Zoltan, Director of Customer Service." Zoltan said he couldn't help unless I paid.

An older American gentleman overheard what I said.

"Zoltan, put this little lady's telephone call on my bill," he said with his Texas drawl. "Honey, I know how you feel. I was robbed last year. What number should I dial?"

I gave him my parents' number. My emotions were released by this stranger who treated me with kindness. As he handed me the phone, I couldn't control my sobs.

"Dad, I was robbed," I said. My father became alarmed, thinking that it was much worse. "No, they only took my wallet. I need you to cancel my credit cards. And call the DMV for a new license."

The dear Texan gave me taxi fare to get home, but instead I went straight to Sue's flat. We had planned to get together that evening anyway. I sat on Sue's bench to remove my shoes, and I told her my story. Once more, the tears flowed. I hadn't expected to feel so stunned by what had happened. That smirking guy on the bus reached inside my purse and took something from me that he had no right to take. I felt violated.

It helped knowing Sue understood and cared. Her big yellow cat, Edward, rubbed against my leg and licked my hand with his sandpaper tongue. Edward the cat, my friend Sue, and a stranger from Texas were God's messengers to comfort me that day.

What About You?

- How do you re-fuel when you're weary of well-doing?

- How can you make time for yourself—to be and not just do? What about time to connect to God?

- How have you needed God's supernatural love for the people you live among?

- We all feel lonely at times, even if our lives are filled with people. How do you handle that?

Chapter 10

OUT OF BUDAPEST

*And the Lord will continually guide you, and satisfy
your desire in scorched places, and give strength to
your bones; and you will be like a watered garden,
and like a spring of water whose waters do not fail.*

—Isaiah 58:11

November 1996, Budapest, Hungary

MONTHS BEFORE I turned 40, I started planning the celebration. I wanted to mark this milestone with joy, neither ignoring the significance nor having an "over-the-hill" party. As I rode the tram downtown, pondering how to accomplish this, the answer became evident.

The six bridges spanning the Danube were strewn with banners proclaiming "40 *Éves*, 1956–1996." Forty years ago, Hungary staged their short-lived revolution against the mighty USSR. I entered the world on their last morning of freedom.

Gaining my inspiration from those banners, I made invitations for my team, drawing the Erzsebet Bridge with a banner stretching from Buda to Pest. I asked them to come to my party

161

wearing outfits from the year 1956. It would be a light-hearted retro birthday.

I spent the day with dear friends—breakfast with Sue and lunch with one of the single guys in the area. The little girls next door made me a cake and sang "Happy Birzday to You" with chocolate frosting smeared on their faces.

When I checked my e-mails, I had many birthday greetings. Steve, my California friend who had stored my things when I first moved overseas, wrote me a sweet note. Steve and I shared this birthday. I wrote him back, sounding a little down. He replied immediately, encouraging me that I had lived the first 40 years of my life well, and God would continue to guide me in the next phase. His words meant so much to me that I printed the e-mail and put it in my folder marked "Special Letters."

I laughed that night, turning 40 with a smile on my face. One woman came to my party in an authentic poodle skirt and her husband's letter jacket. Another guy, a year older than I, rigged up a diaper to wear over his shorts, claiming that's what he wore in 1956. Rock 'n' roll music played as we ate cake and told stories.

I could enjoy that evening because I had dealt with turning 40 several months before, pouring out my heart and my fears before the Lord. I had grieved the death of a dream, and now the mourning had ended. While I still hoped for marriage someday, I had to admit I'd probably never have children. All little girls grow up with the dream of being a mommy, and although I hadn't put my life on hold waiting for that day, I still wanted it. My hope grew stronger each time an older single friend married and had children or adopted them. I believed God could do the impossible, but I still needed to face my present reality squarely.

While I struggled with this loss, I had thoughts I could only speak to a few trusted friends, only to those who had walked my path before. During lonely or exhausted times, when my emotions were most vulnerable, I wondered if God knew I wouldn't be a good mom, and that's why He didn't give me children. Maybe He was protecting them from me. My friends convinced me God didn't think of me that way. Otherwise, why would He have entrusted the care of so many to me over the years? I had raised a brood of spiritual children and grandchildren all over the world.

I memorized Amy Carmichael's words. "May my home on earth be empty, Lord, that Thy home in heaven be made more full." It helped to know that something positive had been born from my lack.

I knew I had much to be thankful for. During my travels, the mothers of young children persuaded me that they were lonelier than single women. Isolated from the language and culture, they felt trapped at home with babies. Their husbands had fulfilling ministries that often excluded them. Some days they didn't even have one adult conversation.

During my time of reflection, I took stock of my life, assessing how I had invested the first part and contemplating what changes I should make for the second. My life so far had been about ministering to people and helping them in their journey to God, and it had been an exciting adventure. I had no regrets. Now, as the second half dawned, I wanted to find my voice in writing, art, and piano. God had given me a modicum of talent and lots of desire, and I needed to cultivate His gift. So far, I hadn't been able to find time or space to do more than decorate my home, write daily journal entries and monthly newsletters, and play the piano occasionally. I didn't expect my schedule to change anytime soon, but I decided to wait on God and trust Him to make a way.

Act Two of my life had commenced.

March 1997, Budapest, Hungary

The phone woke me in the middle of the night. The Americans on our team in Albania had been evacuated to Italy. The anarchy in Albania had escalated, and the Marines escorted our citizens out. The maneuver was named Operation Silver Wake. The team had 15 minutes to load up one backpack apiece and walk to the U.S. Consulate, dodging bullets along the way. Some of their backpacks weighed too much, and the contents were dumped on the Consulate yard. Helicopters whirled them to the coast, and an aircraft carrier shuttled them across the Adriatic to Italy.

Old tribal feuds in Albania had heated up. Catholics in the north, Orthodox in the south, and Muslims throughout the country were killing each other. Their simmering anger over years of subhuman treatment now erupted like a volcano, triggered by collapsed get-rich-quick pyramid schemes. The country had gone mad, washed in a bloodbath. People broke into warehouses for ammunition, and children fired machine guns in the air. Martial law had been imposed, with curfews and no meetings of more than four people allowed.

We brought our teammates to Budapest to wait for the anarchy to end. Four of the American women stayed with me for two months. They had left their flats unoccupied, and looting was certain. The girls mourned over the photographs, letters, and journals they'd forgotten to throw in their backpacks. The Stinters didn't expect to return to Albania. They had been denied the chance to say good-bye to their dearly loved national friends, and that pain cut deepest.

May 1997, Harmony, Maryland

No one met me at the airport when I landed in the States. It was my first furlough since my parents had sold their house in Delaware to travel up to Alaska in their RV. They planned to settle near their grandkids in Arizona. I rented a car and drove to the Eastern Shore of Maryland.

As I pulled into Harmony, the town where I grew up, I knew I had come home. Jan, the woman who had led me to Christ years ago and mentored me spiritually, echoed that. "Harmony will always be your home, Taryn, no matter where you or your parents live." I needed to hear that.

A large map of Eastern Europe hung on the easel. I picked up a marker and drew a vertical line, cutting it in half. "There are two distinct sides to what we consider Eastern Europe. The countries to the left of this line are now referred to as Central Europe. The ones to the right are still called Eastern Europe," I told my friends who had come to Harmony to hear about my ministry.

"First of all, I'd like to tell you about the similarities. People in this part of the world have artists' souls. They are poets, not pragmatists. They have always been oppressed. Before Communism, they were serfs and always under some empire's thumb. They long to be accepted by Western Europe, but before that happens, they have to prove that they have a right to be part of Europe. Each of these countries has its own distinct personality.

"Now for the differences. Remember, these are just broad sweeping generalizations, not meant to offend. Central Europe is Catholic, it's more Western, cleaner and more orderly, the people are quieter and better off economically, they are prouder and more apathetic. Eastern Europe is Eastern Orthodox, more chaotic and dirty, the people are expressive, and the poverty is more severe. The spiritual center of Catholicism is Rome, which is in the West. For Orthodoxy, it's Constantinople or Istanbul, which is in the Middle East. Orthodoxy is dark and mystical, harder for Westerners to understand.

CENTRAL
EUROPE

EASTERN
EUROPE

FORMER
U.S.S.R.

Russia

Belarus

Poland

Czech
Republic

Slovakia

Ukraine

Moldova

Hungary

Slovenia

Croatia

Romania

Bosnia

Serbia

Bulgaria

Montenegro

Macedonia

Albania

"All of these countries speak Slavic languages, with three exceptions: Romania, which is called a Latin island in a Slavic sea; Hungary; and Albania. There seems to be a correlation between affluence and response to the gospel. The poorest countries (Albania, Romania, Moldova, and Ukraine) are the most responsive. They see their neediness more clearly.

"I'm going to start at the top of the map on the Central Europe side and work my way to the bottom," I went on, pointing to Poland. "I love the indomitable spirit of the Poles. Imagine being squeezed between two powerful countries, Germany and Russia, and not losing your identity. Their fierce national pride has never been squelched, and the Communists couldn't stifle religion in the land of the pope. I have been to Chopin concerts where everyone stands, tears in their eyes and hands on their hearts, as they listen to their native son. In Poland, you feel the weight of World War II more than Communism. The War began with the invasion of Warsaw on September 1, 1939. Eighty percent of the city and its inhabitants were destroyed. Poles are haunted by Auschwitz and the innocents who were massacred on their soil.

"I love going to staff meetings in Poland. Everyone has an opinion, and they all speak at once. Poland was the first country we had staff living in, back in the 1970s, when it was behind the Iron Curtain. Today we have 100 staff in six cities, and almost all of them are nationals.

"The next country is the Czech Republic. During Communism, there was a marked contrast when crossing the border from lively Poland to silent Czechoslovakia, where fear dictated that no one would be out on the streets. No Man's Land, now with empty guard towers, stretches a few kilometers between Czechoslovakia and Austria. In 1989, they had the Velvet Revolution; and in 1993, Slovakia left peacefully in the Velvet Divorce.

"Czechs are known to be analytical and critical. At student meetings, when comment cards are handed out to find out reactions to the message of Christ, the students write, 'Your accent hurt my ears.' I'm glad I studied language in a country where they were gracious with my mistakes. Czech is the most Western of our countries and the most apathetic spiritually. It's a hard place for our staff to minister.

"To publicize a talk at the university in Prague before Easter, they made a giant papier-mâché rock with a sign bearing the title of the message, 'Who Moved the Stone?' Someone stole the rock but left the sign. The staff felt discouraged, until they saw the packed room that night. Students came to the talk to find out who moved the papier-mâché stone, and once there, they heard the Easter story.

"Czech's other half is Slovakia. The Slovak Republic wanted to stand on their own even though they didn't have the industry or infrastructure. They are having a harder time economically than Czech, but we're seeing more interest in the gospel. Václav Havel, a former playwright, was the last President of Czechoslovakia. He stepped down when his country split apart and then was re-elected as President of the Czech Republic.

"This year a pizza delivery place opened in Bratislava, the capital. That is exciting news to expatriates. The staff called to order a pizza, and it didn't come. Three nights later, someone knocked on their door. It was the pizza guy. They joked that the slogan should be, 'If it's not there in a week, it'll be free.'"

Hungary came next. I described our successful Youth at the Threshold of Life program. One of our young national staff guys approached the Minister of Education and offered to teach an AIDS awareness and abstinence program in the high schools. The Minister liked it so much, he made it mandatory for every high school student. Teachers all over the country are trained in delivering this curriculum. Both teachers and students hear the gospel and have opportunity for Bible studies.

"The last two countries in Central Europe are Slovenia and Croatia, both independent republics from Yugoslavia. Slovenia left in 1992 without a fight. Croatia's departure that same year was violent.

"Slovenia is tiny. It's the northernmost republic, bordering Austria and Italy," I continued. "It is a perfect jewel, with the Alps and the Adriatic. Slovenes are more subdued than the lively Croats, probably because they're so close to Western Europe. One of my all-time favorite places is Lake Bled, in the mountains. The white Lipizzaner stallions that perform in Vienna came from Slovenia."

I pointed to Croatia on the map, explaining that Serbs and Croats were the same people, with different religions. "Both Serbia and Croatia are guilty of war crimes, both have blood on their hands, but we took Croatia's side, and that helped end the Bosnian war. Franjo Tudjman led the Croats to adopt their old Fascist constitution from before World War II. As a matter of fact, Jasenovač concentration camp sits on their soil, and they have never atoned for their part in the Holocaust.

"Josip Broz Tito, the Communist leader of Yugoslavia, was Croatian, and many claim that's why Croatia is boomerang-shaped to include the stunning Dalmatian coast. Tito treated his people better than the neighboring dictators. He had amazing charisma and somehow managed to hold the six republics together. Once he died, their centuries-old feuds erupted again, leading to the Bosnian War."

I decided I'd better pick up the pace a little, moving on to the Eastern European side, starting at the top again. "I've been talking to you about Romania for years now, so we'll skip to Bulgaria. Bulgaria is sometimes called Little Russia because of their close connection. They use the Cyrillic alphabet, same as Russia. In fact, two Bulgarian monks, Cyril and Methodius, wrote the alphabet. Bulgaria is free of conflict but full of contradiction. It's the only country in Eastern Europe where you don't kiss in greeting. They are not as affectionate or effusive as neighboring countries.

"Next is Yugoslavia. Most people call it Serbia, although the republic of Montenegro is still with them—for now at least. Serbia's roots are Orthodox, but most people actually don't believe in any religion. Russia supported them in the Bosnian War, and their alphabet is also Cyrillic. The Serbian people love to laugh and talk, stay out late at cafés, and sleep in late—just like the Croats. They have a great sense of humor. A couple months ago, students all over Belgrade demonstrated against Slobodan Milošević. Every evening at 7:00, the whole city would try to drown out the state news, shouting, honking horns, and banging silverware on pans. I saw their TV commercial showing the demonstrators drumming with forks and spoons, saying, 'Buy this brand of silverware! Look how tough it is! It doesn't get bent!'

"Last year, in March 1996, I was in Serbia eating Mexican food at the American Consulate, when Congressman Ron Brown's plane went down in Croatia. We watched it on Armed Forces Network. To enter Serbia, I always have a scary border crossing. The guards make you get off the train at the border and go inside a dark building for passport control. You have to leave your luggage unattended on the train, and you never know what the guards might do to you. But God always provides someone to help. I like to call them my angels. This time, I had a tough angel—a Marine deployed to guard the Embassy in Belgrade. He was at the Consulate that night when we watched Armed Forces Network.

"Macedonia is officially named the Former Yugoslav Republic of Macedonia, often written FYROM. Everyone wants Macedonia. It's the next powder keg waiting to be detonated. Serbia, Greece, Albania, Bulgaria, and Turkey all claim this country. But most Macedonians just want to be independent. Mother Teresa is from the capital, Skopje. She is an ethnic Albanian.

"Bosnia and Albania are exceptions," I explained. "They are a mixture of three religions—Islam, Orthodoxy, and Catholicism. That's why their people can't get along. Bosnia is a ravaged war zone. Sarajevo used to be a beautiful mountain city. Remember, the Winter Olympics were held there in 1984. Here's a bit of trivia: the Austrian Archduke Ferdinand was murdered by a Serb in Sarajevo, which started World War I."

I ended my presentation with an update on the anarchy in Albania. "Any questions?"

"We hear about the Balkans all the time in the news," someone said. "Can you tell us what that is exactly?"

I picked up the marker again, this time drawing a horizontal line across it. "The area below this line is the Balkans. It stretches from Istanbul, Turkey to Istria—the Istrian peninsula of former Yugoslavia. It includes Albania, all the former Yugoslav republics, Bulgaria, Romania, and Greece. This is where all the conflict is right now in my part of the world."

I told them that the best description I had read of the Balkans was penned by C. L. Sulzberger in *A Long Row of Candles*. I had it in my notes. "It is a gay peninsula filled with sprightly people who ate peppered foods, drank strong liquors, wore flamboyant clothes, loved and murdered easily, and had a splendid talent for starting wars."

"Many of you remember that Yugoslavia was the first country I ever visited outside of the United States, back in 1986. That summer mission project changed the course of my life and is why I returned to Eastern Europe. Yugoslavs had more freedoms—they were not aligned with the USSR—yet it has always been one of the least spiritually responsive countries. The first student I shared my testimony with that summer was Gordana Miletič. She gave all the typical responses. 'I am an atheist. Only old women believe those fables.' And yet Christ won her over shortly after the summer project ended. Gordana has been on our staff since 1990 and is one of my dearest friends.

171

Because that country has been on my heart for so many years, I am deeply grieved when I see what's happened.

"The word Yugoslavia means South Slavs, and it used to include six republics. We've talked about four of them breaking away (Slovenia, Croatia, Bosnia, and Macedonia) and two remaining as the Federal Republic of Yugoslavia (Serbia and Montenegro). When Croatia and Bosnia declared their independence, the Bosnian War started. That was in March 1992. It lasted until November 1995. Now the Serbs and Albanians are fighting each other over an autonomous province within Serbia that's filled with ethnic Albanians. I'm sure you've heard of Kosovo in the news."

I saw some eyes start to glaze over. It was time to call it an evening.

Fall 1997, Out of Budapest

I returned to Budapest to find that our staff had gone home to Albania, so I flew to Tirana to check on them. The destruction I witnessed shocked me—burned-out hulls of cars and glass from demolished buildings littered the streets and fields. Albanians did this themselves, destroying the little they had.

Each night I heard gunshots, much closer than I preferred. A few weeks before, Democratic Deputy Hajdari had been shot and wounded by a Socialist inside the Parliament chamber, while it was in session.

The national staff, who had not been evacuated, repeated the same refrain to me. "Praise God! None of our girls were taken."

"What do you mean by 'taken'?" I asked, afraid to know.

"None of them were raped."

As my plane lifted to depart, I sat glued to the window. I drank in the gorgeous mountains and sparkling blue sea, in sharp contrast to the demolition and poverty. I sensed all creation being held in bondage, along with so many of the people below me, groaning to be set free, as Paul described in Romans. I envisioned the day when all will be made right, when the mountains will break forth in shouts of joy, and the trees will clap their hands. Some day Albania will truly shine. For now, I smiled, knowing that hundreds of lives had already been freed by Christ.

Our area kept growing. Besides new national staff joining every year, four former republics of the USSR were added to our numbers. With the increase of Ukraine, Belarus, Moldova, and Russia, our area now included 17 countries and 12 time zones—half of the Northern Hemisphere. We gained over 200 more staff to care for.

I needed to study up on these countries. At least the Eastern Orthodox religion they shared would not be new to me. I read Winston Churchill's statement from 1939: "The Soviet Union is a riddle wrapped up in a mystery inside an enigma." It seemed to still be true today.

The satellite countries of the Eastern Bloc had been under Communism's thumb for 45 years. For the Soviet republics, it had been almost 75 years, since 1917. After decades of speaking Russian, they were now re-claiming their national identities and re-learning their national languages.

I decided to start by visiting the most familiar. Years ago, the region of Romania called Moldova was cut in half along the Prut River. The western part, where the painted monasteries stand, remained with Romania, and the eastern part became one of the 15 republics of the USSR. Many ethnic Russians were shipped there to intermarry with the people and squelch any attempts at independence. The official language became Russian; but now ethnic Romanians in Moldova were learning Romanian for the first time. I could communicate without a translator.

I nervously carried the salary for the Moldovan national staff in my money belt—5,000 in U.S. dollars. It looked as though my plane had landed in Bucharest in 1990. Armed military men lined the parapets. There were no lights in the airport or outside on the streets. Concrete block buildings stretched on for miles.

I joined a team of Romanian staff and students in Chisinău, the capital, to train Moldovans in basic ministry skills. Daniela, the women's leader for Romania, and Nicu and Cristina, newly-married and newly on staff, came to minister to their long-lost cousins. I remembered meeting Daniela as a baby believer in 1990, and leading Cristina to Christ in her dorm room in 1992. Angelica welcomed us at the hotel, with her sweet spirit and big heart. She had the daunting task of coordinating the fledgling ministry in Moldova. Daniela and I spent much of the week mentoring her.

The temperatures had dipped abnormally low. We had no heat or hot water in our hotel, but that didn't chill the enthusiasm of the 100 Moldovans gathered to learn. We wore every layer we brought to bed, and we still shivered. The Romanians felt sorry for their neighbors and seemed to forget that conditions in their own country were just as bad a few years ago. Many felt burdened with the need for staff and started praying seriously about moving to Moldova to help.

"I don't know if I could live in such difficult conditions. We have so much more in Romania that I would have to give up," Cristina said. "Terena, how did you do it? How did you leave America to come to us?"

"Cristina, seriously it wasn't that hard. Sure, there were moments, but I knew that God called me, and He provided everything I needed. And you guys made it all worthwhile." I looked into her eyes. "You know, wherever God calls you and Nicu, He'll take care of you, too."

My next trip was to Kiev, Ukraine for a staff conference held in an austere Soviet sanatorium. Ukraine was the Bible Belt of the USSR. The underground churches grew while suffering under persecution; even grew stronger because of it. This reminded me of Romania, and I at once felt at home.

Oksana, the women's leader, juggled more responsibilities than I could imagine. Besides coordinating countrywide ministries and training staff, she was also mother to her teenage sister. They had been orphaned due to alcoholism. Usually single staff in the States don't have to hurry home to cook for a rebellious teenager and make her do her homework.

When the nuclear plant in Chernobyl exploded in 1986, the winds blew north to Belarus, contaminating one-third of their population. Chernobyl stood on the site of a Holocaust killing field, and later, Stalin's mass killings as part of his collectivization campaign. Earlier, the Holodomor famine spread throughout Ukraine in 1932, caused by deliberate Soviet policies. The Soviets purposely starved thousands of Ukrainians to death. Evil had reigned in that geography. I could taste the oppressiveness.

From Ukraine, I flew to Belarus. Our pilot walked down the aisle, greeting passengers before take-off. I noticed his nametag had the word "Igor" handwritten in pencil. I guess he didn't have job security. Outside the capital, Minsk, a pile of ashes called "Glory" stood by the road, where German and Russian armies had collided at the end of WWII. Belarus was the Russian Front. The ashes of bodies and burned-out villages from that fiery meeting remained untouched. One out of every four Belarussians had died in the war.

I hadn't known that Lee Harvey Oswald lived in Minsk in the early 1960s. He became a Communist, defected to the USSR, and returned to America to assassinate President Kennedy. I stayed with the Stint girls in the apartment of his girlfriend, Marina Prusakova. A copy of *Oswald's Tale*, written and autographed by Norman Mailer, sat on the coffee table. I thought it should be behind glass.

The team told me that recently hundreds of young college students, mostly girls in high heels, had been trampled to death as they ran from an outdoor concert into a metro station to escape a hailstorm. The loss of life in Belarus shook me.

Curiously, I didn't have to go through passport control on my way to Russia. Flying from Belarus, closely aligned with Mother Russia, was considered a domestic flight. I arrived at the airport along with Krystyna, the women's leader in Poland. Sergei met us at the gate, holding a sign saying "Stint." He shuttled us through the snowy streets to Brad and Anya's flat, where the Stinters began to assemble. Our flight to Siberia would not leave until midnight.

Krystyna and I walked to Red Square and ate American pizza outside the entrance. That seemed odd to me, somehow. Stripped of much of its power, Red Square still awed me as I walked across the massive brick expanse, imagining soldiers goose-stepping in their long wool coats and fur caps. I admired St. Basil's variegated onion domes, Lenin's Mausoleum, and the nearby Kremlin on the Moskva River, with its four palaces and four cathedrals dominating the skyline.

I stood freely in the country that held Eastern Europe in its stranglehold for so many years, the nation that inspired fear in Americans' hearts and served as the backdrop for countless spy novels. I could see that Red Square affected Krystyna much more than it did me. Russia had been the hated enemy all of her life. Russia hadn't existed half a world away for her; it had been everywhere, controlling her daily reality.

Most of the Russian people were victims, I reminded myself. The government enslaved so much of the world, including its own people, in poverty, fear, and lack of basic freedoms. Russians longed for freedom as much as citizens of the satellite countries.

I thought of the pogroms against the Jews, the execution of Czar Nicholas and his family, Lenin and the Bolsheviks staging the October Revolution in 1917, Stalin exterminating 20 million people—many more than Hitler. The wind chapped my face and lips, the only part of me exposed to the elements. It was

My first visit to Red Square in Moscow.

just November, but the chill was bitter, and it didn't come from the air alone.

177

The vast country of Russia encompasses 10 time zones. We flew all the way to Ulan-Ude in Siberia and only covered five time zones—half of the country. I arrived in the land of gulags to train all the Stint teams scattered across Russia. Although the thermometer registered even lower temperatures than Moscow, it didn't feel as cold, due to the dry climate in the steppes. The architecture of the city looked European, with a gigantic head of Lenin as the gathering place in the center of the city. However, the Buryat people were Asian, descended from neighboring

Training conference in Siberia for Stint teams throughout Russia.

Mongolia. The women were tall and gorgeous, with flawless complexions. They wore beautiful, long mink coats and hats.

For some reason, the men seemed to be shorter, squatter, and more weathered. Couples reminded me of Boris and Natasha Badenov from the Rocky and Bullwinkle cartoons.

We connected with many Siberian students that week. Siberians had less freedom and endured more persecution than Muscovites. Yet despite that, and in the middle of the remotest nowhere, Jesus' love still reached out and captivated hearts.

"A few years ago, a Buryat girl joined my class, and she told me about Jesus," Lena said. "She was first person I knew who believed in Jesus, until team from America came, that is. I told my family, and now all of us are followers of Christ. This summer, I will go to Mongolia to tell people about Jesus, because they need chance to hear." Lena's eyes moistened. "God is so good to me. I know He's crazy for me!"

Our staff and students around the area were catching the vision, not just of reaching their own country for Christ, but of carrying the good news to the world. Albanians were going to Turkey, Romanians to Moldova and China, Czechs to Serbia, and Poles to Russia and Belarus. My joy could hardly be contained.

Ministry in Central and Eastern Europe exhilarated me, and I felt like a well-watered garden. I could handle anything.

What About You?

- How can you take control and plan so that your next milestone (birthday, anniversary, or remembrance of a sad time) will be meaningful?

- What gives you joy?

- Examine your life. How have you invested it so far? What changes can you make for the next phase?

Chapter 11

WHERE THIEVES
DO NOT BREAK IN
AND STEAL

*"Do not lay up for yourselves treasures upon earth, where
moth and rust destroy, and where thieves break
in and steal, but lay up for yourselves treasures
in heaven, where neither moth nor rust destroys,
and where thieves do not break in or steal;
for where your treasure is, there will
your heart be also."*

—Matthew 6:19–21

January 1998, Budapest, Hungary

THE SILENCE SEEMED out-of-place as I unlocked the
iron gate and started up the walkway to my apartment.
Usually the dogs next door barked at me, but they weren't in
their yard. I had been ringing in the New Year at my friend
Rilla's flat, and it was about an hour into 1998. Rilla's landlord
had closed his dog up inside the house because the fireworks
frightened him. He claimed that all Hungarians did the same
on New Year's Eve.

181

I had my hand extended, key ready, reaching for my doorknob, when I noticed. There was no doorknob. A square hole had been neatly cut out of my front door. The door swung freely, and I glimpsed the kitchen cabinets standing wide open. That's when my mind finally connected with reality.

I had been robbed.

Afraid to enter alone, I raced next door to Agota and Gezá's flat and pounded on their door. Gezá opened up, and I blurted out what had happened. He quickly telephoned the police.

"Do not go inside. Wait here," he said. "The thieves may still be there. The police will come soon."

Agota made us coffee, and I waited in their kitchen. My grandmother's diamond ring filled my thoughts. Before moving, my parents had given me my inheritance from their safe deposit box, thinking the ring would be safer with me in Budapest than inside their RV during their cross-country travels. The engagement ring reminded me of my sweet grandmother. Made about 1925, the diamonds sat up tall in their platinum setting. Grandmom had never owned anything lovelier.

I proudly wore it everyday, except for this day. The ring had begun to catch on my gloves, and I feared the prongs had loosened. I needed my gloves in the chilly night air, so I took my ring off before I left, setting it on my dresser. It would have been the first thing any thief would notice.

Still, it didn't hurt to pray. As I sipped the coffee, I repeated in my mind, "God, please cause Grandmom's ring to still be there."

The police didn't arrive for almost an hour, about 2:00 in the morning. Gezá explained the situation to the two officers and translated for me. They told us to stand outside as they entered the apartment to check each room.

Even if the thieves had somehow missed the ring, the policemen could easily have scooped it into a pocket. I had to trust the officers.

After several minutes, the detective arrived. He beckoned to us to follow him inside. He led me into each room and asked me what was missing. Grandmom's ring was not there. In fact, my entire jewelry box had been taken. My laptop computer and printer belonging to the office, my CD player, microwave, camera, television, and video player were all gone.

Every drawer sat ajar. The thieves had carefully combed through all my belongings. My credit cards from the States, useless in Budapest, were laid out on my bed in a straight, orderly line. Department stores and gas companies that didn't exist in Eastern Europe had been passed up. Luckily, my Visa card remained safe inside my purse.

The officers dusted the entire house for fingerprints, while the detective motioned to us to sit at the kitchen table. He wrote a few notes and then looked up, studying me.

"It was the Russian Mafia."

"How do you know?" I asked through Gezá.

"The Mafia only takes electronics and jewelry. They steal items that can be carried easily and sold quickly. If it was gypsies, they would have trashed the place and taken clothes or anything that caught their eye. The door was cut professionally, one of their trademarks. The Mafia comes in groups of at least three. One person is the look-out. The others go through each room methodically. They do not rush. They left through the back door."

I had noticed that the patio door stood wide open.

"Do you know anyone in the Mafia?" he asked me.

"No, of course not," I said. Gezá assured him I was a good, quiet girl, and I did not run in those circles.

"If you had been home, they would have killed you."

After almost three hours, the police officers left as the new day began to break. Gezá, who had stayed up all night to help, instructed me to push my hutch against the door after he left.

I could no longer lock myself in. I couldn't warm up in my flat either. All night, both doors had remained open. I cranked up the heat, put on my warmest layers, and burrowed under my down comforter.

My first thoughts were of thankfulness that my treasure wasn't tied up in things but sat secure in heaven. Someday I will live in a place where there are no thieves. I praised God that He had protected me and my neighbors from harm, glad I hadn't come home early from the party. I thanked Him by faith, remembering that I am to express gratitude in all things, affirming that He somehow allowed this to enter my life through the filter of His great hands of love. I cried as I thanked the Lord for the gift of letting me borrow Grandmom's beautiful ring for all those months, thanking Him especially for having been blessed with such a sweet grandmother.

I recited words of comfort that dwelled deep inside, as my eyes refused to close. "Do not fear, for I am with you. Do not anxiously look about you, for I am your God. I will strengthen you, surely I will help you, surely I will uphold you with My righteous right hand" (Isaiah 41:10).

His Word calmed my heart. I rehearsed the well-worn promises of Psalm 23, scrunching lower under my comforter, wrapping myself in God's love.

"The Lord is my shepherd, I shall not want. He makes me lie down in green pastures. He leads me beside quiet waters. He restores my soul. He guides me in the paths of righteousness for His name's sake. Even though I walk through the valley of the shadow of death, I fear no evil; for Thou art with me. They rod and Thy staff, they comfort me. Thou dost prepare a table before me in the presence of my enemies. Thou hast anointed my head with oil. My cup overflows. Surely goodness and lovingkindness will follow me all the days of my life; and I will dwell in the house of the Lord forever."

As sleep eluded me, hot tears escaped from my eyes, and my body convulsed in silent sobs.

In shock all day, I never once thought about anything as mundane as eating. I was sure the burglary had been a nightmare. I only had to look at the hole in my front door or the black smear of fingerprint goop on every surface to realize that wasn't true.

I thought surely God would prove Himself mighty by returning my ring to me. Maybe the thieves would be apprehended and dramatically turn from crime, giving their lives to Christ. That's how I would write that script. Perhaps one day I would spot the ring glistening along the side of the road as I walked to the bus. I had read of people finding a family heirloom washed up on the sands of the beach. God would do the same for me, I just knew it.

Throughout the day, I kept remembering other pieces of jewelry that had been stolen. I thought of my first ring, a heart-shaped birthstone, given to me by my aunt in elementary school and re-sized recently. My uncle who died young had chosen a bracelet for me in Korea, where he served as peacekeeper after the war. I had nothing else from Uncle Wade. An old boyfriend had given me a jade set. I didn't care about him anymore, but I liked remembering that, once upon a time, I had a boyfriend. My other grandmother's pearl necklace, lapis earrings I bought in Turkey, a fake ruby ring I bartered for in the Cotswolds, my teenage charm bracelet, all were gone. Each piece reminded me of a certain person or a distinct time in my life. The Mafia hadn't just taken my jewelry; they had taken pieces of my heart. Each memory stabbed me afresh.

Agota stopped by to check on me. I told her that I had hope that the ring would turn up. Maybe the thieves had a hole in their bag, and it fell out in our yard. Later I stood at the window and saw her four little girls combing the yard with a rake and a flashlight. They were looking for my ring. The girls did find my useless can of pepper spray, a joke left behind by my burglars.

The police asked me to come in to file an official report and bring a complete list of every missing object—but not today or tomorrow because of the New Year's holiday. They wouldn't start searching until after I filed the report. When we arrived, the police told Gezá and me that the Mafia works quickly, and since my robbery happened three days before, they were sure my things had been sold. My frustration mounted. *So why did they make me wait?* They suggested I search pawn shops myself. The detective asked me again if I had any connections to the Mafia.

I did. I had forgotten. Eszter, the Hungarian secretary in our office, had recently separated from a man involved in the Mafia. Janos had served as a liaison to get our cars fixed. I had turned over my Passat to him to work on the electric windows. When he brought it back, along with a hefty bill, I noticed that it had been driven hundreds of kilometers.

I called Janos in to my office and confronted him. I told him I would warn the others. He cursed at me. He made a lot of money from the Americans, and he didn't want to be exposed and lose the income. I told Janos I didn't appreciate his language and asked him to leave. As I held the door open for him, Grandmom's ring caught his eye.

"That is a beautiful ring. How much is it worth?" he asked.

"It's none of your business," I said.

Eszter begged me not to turn in Janos. I relented, against my better judgment. Janos's disgruntled clients had thrown rocks, covered in death threats, through her window. I didn't want to add to the difficulties for her and the children.

The police suspected the Mafia had been watching me for weeks. Once again I had been stalked and violated. Something had been taken from me by force, against my will.

I couldn't sleep for weeks. Even after my landlord finally replaced the lock and installed an alarm, I still didn't feel safe. I couldn't let down my guard at home, still shaken from the trauma and saddened by the loss.

I e-mailed friends all over the world, asking them to pray for me. They responded immediately. God wrapped His arms of love tightly around me through my friends, family, and ministry partners. They felt heartsick for me and understood my sleeplessness. Many validated the fact that I needed to grieve this loss. Only a few people made unnecessary comments like, "Look on the bright side. It's only things."

I knew I had lost things and not people. I knew there is no comparison between a robbery and a death. But I still felt legitimately sad and uneasy.

Teammates invited me to their homes for dinner, trying to coax me away from the scene of the crime. I didn't know why, but I didn't want to go. One family, the Hyatts, came to my place with a fondue pot and all the fixings. We had a wonderful evening together. They asked me all about the robbery. Their son played my piano as the cheese bubbled. We laughed together and had a delightful conversation. They truly ministered to me.

Afterwards, I thought about what the Hyatts had done for me. They helped me feel like my home was a good place to be. I enjoyed being at home that evening. They brought laughter back. I needed to talk about what had happened, and they helped me process it. I realized the reason I didn't want to go out is that I didn't want to come home alone again, after dark. Logical or not, I feared a repeat of the other night.

The Hyatts knew what I needed, because they had been robbed themselves. I tucked this away in my heart to be able to pull it out someday myself, to comfort someone else in need.

About six weeks after the break-in, I had a break-through time alone with God. I forgave everyone with whom I felt angry. I absolved the thieves, the police who didn't work very hard on my case, my landlord who took his time fixing my lock, my teammates who didn't demonstrate care for me, people who made stupid and hurtful comments, and myself for taking the ring off that night. I even forgave God for allowing my precious things to be taken when He knew I would have to deal with it alone. I released healing tears and felt a burden removed from my shoulders.

I had moved through most of the stages of grief: denial, depression, anger, and now acceptance. I had skipped the bargaining phase. I guess I knew I could never be good enough to live up to a bargain with God, so I didn't try.

As I traveled the next few months, the staff I visited ministered to me in practical ways. Krystyna helped me buy my first new earrings in Poland, a crystal pair that cost about five dollars. Velislava and I went shopping in Bulgaria for a marcasite ring. Nikki helped me pick out a handmade silver bracelet in Albania. My new jewelry meant almost as much to me as the pieces I had lost. It represented these new friends and their countries which I dearly loved.

I had wept with the staff for a few years now as they poured out the struggles of their hearts to me. This year they cried with me. Our bonds became even stronger.

How could I think about leaving them?

I knew in my heart that it was time to go back. I had reached my limit of major traumas that I could deal with alone. After being raided by the police in Bucharest, stalked in Cluj, pick-pocketed and now robbed in Budapest, I couldn't handle anymore. As much as I loved living and ministering in Eastern Europe, I felt drained by the constant traveling and giving to others. My supply needed replenishing. I needed to receive for a while. I had decided years ago that I didn't want to wait until my parents were in a nursing home to return. As they neared 70, my time to leave grew closer.

Besides, I had replaced myself with nationals. Our area had become so large that we planned to split it into four regions. In each region, a national woman was trained and ready to take on more responsibility. Together, they could assume my position. I couldn't think of any good reason for a foreigner to stay when nationals were equipped.

I knew better than to make a major decision in the middle of an emotional crisis. For the next several months, I sought God through His Word and being still before Him, asking Him what He wanted for me. I processed aloud with dear godly friends, who encouraged me with the rightness of the path unfolding before me.

As the fall of 1998 began, I had labored over my decision long enough, convinced that God wanted me to return to the States. I made it official. I wouldn't leave until spring 2000. I told my team and the leadership women throughout the area, preparing them for their need to step up.

The final 18 months proved ample time to focus on my priority—cultivating relationships with the countrywide leadership women. Every trip I made had a double purpose. I took a different national women's leader with me to visit each country. Slavica from Serbia traveled with me to Poland to be with Krystyna, and Velislava from Bulgaria met me in Romania to visit Daniela. We had time to talk as we traveled, opportunities to model ministry, and a chance to see the friendship cemented between the two national women.

January 1999, Canary Islands

I dug my toes in the soft, white sand, marveling at how I came to be in the Canary Islands in the middle of winter.

After Christmas, we hosted a huge conference at Lake Balaton, Hungary. All of the Campus Crusade staff throughout the 17-country area, numbering 900, came for a week of meetings. The conference room resembled the United Nations, with 14 translation booths set up in the back. The amount of work involved to put this on was so immense that our director had given us headquarters staff the week off afterward.

In the midst of a bitter cold snap, the idea of going to a tropical island kept surfacing in my thoughts. *That's ridiculous.* I stuffed my dream down deep, but not so deep that it couldn't resurface when friends from church told me about an incredible package deal to the Canary Islands. The day before the conference, I hurried to reserve my space for the week off. The round-trip flight from Budapest and the hotel for a week totaled just $200.

I arrived in Tenerife, the largest of Spain's Canary Islands, situated off the coast of Morocco, armed with my Bible, journal, and an empty notebook. The second part of my decision weighed on me: I still didn't know where to go when I left Europe. I had gathered information and advice from trusted friends about several options, all in different cities. This week, I determined to choose one.

I luxuriated in my week alone with the Lord, praying and resting in the tropical splendor. By day, I explored the beaches and volcanoes, returning to my room at night to pore over my list of criteria for my new home and place of ministry. By the middle of the week, two options were tied for first place. One was in Florida and the other in New York, a city I had always loved. The ministry opportunities were equally good, although very different. How could I know which to pursue?

As I strolled along the glistening sand, I asked God for wisdom. The sun warmed me as the brilliant flowers and thundering surf invigorated me. *I love this scene.*

I sensed God speaking to my heart. *Taryn, you love a tropical paradise.*

At that moment, I knew. I needed to choose Florida. Florida looked like this. God brought me to the ocean to remind me that He created me with a delight for the sea—and to refresh my soul.

March 1999, Budapest, Hungary

We had talked about it for years, and now the day had come for my brother's family to visit. Kurt, Susie, Alex, Mark, and Lisa would stay with me for a couple of weeks.

The heating system in my Passat took its last breath on the drive from the airport. Two blocks from my flat, black smoke billowed inside the car. We unloaded the luggage and carried it the rest of the way. While Susie unpacked, Kurt and the boys pushed the Passat a few blocks downhill to my mechanic's. I couldn't afford to have him repair the entire heating system, so I promised never to use my heater again. That included the defroster. It poured the day we drove to the villages along the Danube Bend. Kurt sat in the front seat armed with towels, constantly wiping the inside of the windshield so I could see. That doesn't happen in a typical guided tour of Hungary.

For home-school assignments, the kids had to write in their journals each day about what they had seen and done. We visited grand castles, explored caves, walked across ancient bridges, and stayed in an empty villa once frequented by Hungary's last Communist President. Lisa, at seven years old, wrote that she most loved watching *Tom and Jerry* cartoons at Aunt Taryn's house.

The day they arrived, the NATO campaign against Serbia began. Hungary had just been accepted into NATO, and the people felt used, convinced that Clinton only wanted them because they bordered Serbia. Hungary had to participate in bombing Novi Sad, the northern part of Serbia where ethnic Hungarians lived. The bombing began March 23, 1999 and lasted for 11 weeks. My friends in Belgrade endured 79 nights of horror.

Each morning I devoured their e-mails, thankful they had survived another night. Tanja had a baby during this time, with no hospital and no clean water. Every night, Jelena had to carry her mother, who was dying of lung cancer, and her grandmother to the basement bomb shelter. Some nights they didn't make it down the stairs in time and had to huddle together in their flat. Her mother gave her life to Christ one night as they listened to the explosions and watched the fires outside. She died a few weeks later.

NATO struck out against Serbia in an attempt to end the crisis in Kosovo. A half-million refugees poured into Albania, with its population of only three million. Rather than meet with students on campus, our staff and students in Tirana now ministered to the displaced Kosovans living in refugee camps. Warm meals and Christ's love were freely given to the traumatized Kosovans.

September 1999, Lake Bled, Slovenia

The capstone of my years in Budapest, the first-ever retreat for our countrywide women leaders, took place at Lake Bled, Slovenia. The women converged at my apartment in Budapest from all corners of our area, over the space of several days. Oksana arrived first to get her visa for Slovenia. Krystyna, Velislava, and Daniela came the next day. Gordana, Jennifer, and Anya made it the day before our retreat. We had a short slumber party and arose early to catch our 6:00 train the next morning.

We met Mary from my headquarters team at the train station, and the nine of us boarded our all-day train. I had 13 train tickets with me. We would meet the others in Slovenia.

Andrea and Aniko would travel by car from Hungary, Cyd would fly from Albania, and Slavica was coming by bus from Serbia.

As soon as our train pulled out of Budapest, we gathered in one compartment to pray together, committing our week to the Lord. We had our purses with us and assigned one of the women to keep an eye on our other compartment. Still, someone crept in and slipped my camera, which I had bought to replace the one the Mafia had stolen, out of the side flap in my suitcase. I had now been robbed three times in Hungary. After having my apartment vandalized, another camera didn't matter that much. My first thought was relief that this happened to me, and not to any of the national women who had less means to replace anything stolen.

Soon we reached the Croatian border. Our train would barely dip into Croatia before entering Slovenia, but Oksana from Ukraine and Anya from Russia didn't have visas to enter Croatia. The conductor evicted them from the train. I quickly asked Gordana, who grew up in Yugoslavia and knew her way to Slovenia, to get off and help them. As Oksana and Anya looked on helplessly from the platform, I scribbled our hotel name and address and telephone numbers of our travel agent and the staff in Slovenia. I slipped it into Gordana's hand and hugged her before she jumped off.

The fierceness of the spiritual battle hinted that this could be a significant week; otherwise the enemy wouldn't bother. The six of us remaining on the train prayed fervently for our friends' protection. Seven of our group, more than half, were now missing.

The first of those, Slavica, waved her welcome as our train pulled into Ljubljana, the pristine capital. Our travel agent met us and drove us to our mountain lake at Bled. Once we settled into our hotel, Andrea and Aniko walked in. Cyd showed up later from the airport.

A little before midnight, our travel agent called. Gordana, Anya, and Oksana were safe at the Ljubljana bus station. He would escort them to us. I hurried to tell the others the good news, so they could rest peacefully and sleep in.

When we gathered together the next day, each traveling group described their adventure getting to Bled. Oksana had everyone in stitches. I planned a relaxed schedule for the week. Every day, we worshipped God and took turns sharing our present situations, our hopes, dreams, and struggles. We prayed as a group for each woman after her turn. Our worship continued as we strolled around the idyllic lake, hiked up to the medieval castle on the hill, or rode the *pletna* boat to the island church.

Slavica took her turn sharing one evening at the Grand Hotel, where we had gone for their famous cream cake. She recounted the NATO bombings of Serbia, which had ended in June.

"Here I sleep like baby. At home I cannot sleep. I am haunted by nightmares. I close my eyes, and I relive it all. The destruction each morning. The noise. The fear."

We encircled our sister, wrapping our arms around her and sobbing with her, as we prayed for her healing and asked God to heal Serbia.

I guided our discussions about deepening our spiritual intimacy with God, shepherding our women in their spiritual development, and growing as a person and leader in our gifted-ness. The women were real about the joys and frustrations of their positions. We talked about how to be more effective without burning out or sacrificing passion, how to last in ministry for a lifetime.

Our sublime week ended too soon. The last evening, we praised God, recounting the wonder of 10 years ago that month, when He did the impossible and brought freedom to each country in Eastern Europe. When the revolutions began in 1989, Gordana and Krystyna were the only nationals in our group who were believers. We thanked God for each

194

National women's leadership retreat at Lake Bled, Slovenia.

other's salvation, the growth in our lives, and the growth in the ministries in our countries, acknowledging that only God could have done that.

The next morning, we left Slovenia. Andrea and Aniko took Oksana and Anya in the car, driving a longer route directly into Hungary, bypassing the problem border with Croatia. We all met up at my flat again, this time for a much more mellow night's sleep.

Our time together did not disappoint my sky-high expectations. We grew in our love for each other and our commitment to God's work. We even came home refreshed spiritually.

Leaving Eastern Europe was the hardest thing I ever had to do. I grieved as though someone had died. Europe was a person to me. Indeed Europe stood for many people to me—people I fiercely loved. Europe accepted me and helped me soar. She became the home I was born to inhabit. I didn't know how I could live apart from her. I felt empty and lost.

In my last year, every time I visited one of my countries, I said good-bye. By the end, I was completely wrung out emotionally after leaving so many times from so many places. The farewells were painful but necessary, a bittersweet affirmation of friendship. I realized that it would not hurt so badly if I had kept people at a distance, and so I embraced the sorrow, while welcoming the relief from sadness that sometimes broke through.

February 2000, Romania

For my final shepherding trip, I traveled to the country closest to my heart. Romania had also been the venue of my inaugural trip, making identical bookends to my five years in this role.

I visited the staff in Bucharest and Cluj, saying good-bye not only to the people but also to the special places I loved. My plane from Cluj included me and a *fotbal* team, whose game going into overtime delayed things. That meant that my flight into Băneasa, Bucharest's domestic airport, would be late. I had to shuttle directly to Otopeni, the international airport down the road, for my return flight to Budapest. I made the flight crew aware of my predicament.

When our Tarom plane touched down at Băneasa, a representative met us on the tarmac, at the bottom of the steps. "Domnişoara Ree-kard-sohn," she cried, waving her arms frantically. "Come with me. *Hai.* Hurry."

She grabbed my hand and pulled me into a van beside the plane. Before the door shut, I heard the tires squeal, and we were

196

off. The driver careened around curves, making sure his precious cargo (me) made it to Otopeni on time. He kept blowing his horn, either warning people that we were coming or celebrating the new speed record he set that day. I didn't know which. My eyes were tightly closed.

At the airport, a Tarom man took his turn in the relay. He grabbed my arm as we sprinted through ticket counters, yelling, "Get out of the way." We ran past Customs, waving my passport and ticket. I felt like royalty. I noticed a blur of colorful shops and modern, computerized equipment. It looked nothing like the Otopeni I first met 10 years before.

We made it. I boarded and settled into a spacious leather seat. I leaned back and smiled to myself, taking deep breaths to slow my heartbeat. I couldn't have planned a more perfect way to leave Romania.

What About You?

- Where is your treasure? How would you feel if your dearest possessions were stolen or lost in a fire?

- Have you ever been angry at God for something He allowed to happen? Express those feelings to God. He can take it. He already knows how you feel, so why not tell Him?

- Do you have a decision facing you? It may not be the Canary Islands, but is there a quiet place you can go to hear from God? How will you seek His heart in the matter?

Chapter 12

COMING "HOME"

*"I will lead the blind by ways they have not known, along
unfamiliar paths I will guide them;
I will turn the darkness into light before them and
make the rough places smooth.
These are the things I will do; I will not forsake them."*

—Isaiah 42:16 (NIV)

March 2000, Budapest, Hungary

I PLOPPED DOWN on the step between the second and third floors of my apartment, holding my coffee mug and purse. From this perch, I could oversee all four rooms in my flat. The day I had dreaded for more than a year had finally arrived. Today was moving day.

A British company came to pack up everything for me, load it into a half-sized container, and take care of the customs paperwork at each border, all for a reasonable price. That brisk day in March, I watched my belongings get bubble-wrapped and jammed into boxes. Several times throughout the day, I had to rescue my purse from one of the boxes, even my mug with a few sips of coffee still inside. Luckily, I had stored my bedding and two suitcases next door at Agota's.

My things left one month before I did. I planned to live in my empty flat, using my landlord's furniture and only the barest necessities. In two months my container would arrive in Florida, traveling first by truck, then train, and lastly on an ocean liner.

With all my traveling around Europe, I had earned the very first frequent flier award given by the Hungarian airline Málev. Soon after the movers left, I redeemed it by flying to the Costa del Sol in Spain. By now, vacationing alone felt normal. Besides, I didn't want to talk to anyone. I needed this week to dwell with my memories in a beautiful setting.

I explored the rocky paths down the cliff that opened up to the glistening Mediterranean. In the quaint town of Nerja, I moved from one café table to another, remembering, listening, and writing. By the end of the week, the blank journal I had packed burst with reflections about my decade in Eastern Europe. I wrote about the times God had met me and I had seen evidence of His provision of grace and strength, remembering my plea from Vienna as I began this adventure 10 years before. His fingerprints were visible everywhere. I wanted to leave Europe with a full and grateful heart and a rested body.

I returned to Budapest for my last good-byes there. The day before my plane left for the States, at lunch with a friend, thieves stole my purse from under the table, with my leg through the strap. Now the total count of my robberies in Budapest equaled four. While Cindy and I chatted with a young couple who approached our table, an unseen person cut the strap and ran off with my purse, undoubtedly working in cahoots.

In case any doubts about leaving lingered, God used this robbery to say to me, *Just go*. My passport and tickets were safe in my apartment, but neighbors had to let me in, because my keys had been inside my purse. I had to board the plane for America with cash my friend Cindy gave me.

Agota urged me not to think poorly of Hungarians after all my robberies.

"Don't worry," I said. "I will always love this country." And I meant it. Romania would forever be my first love, but God had answered my prayer by giving me deep affection for Hungary as well. She had also become home to me.

Agota volunteered to take me to the airport the next day, but I had already reserved my faithful Mini-Busz. She and her girls helped carry my luggage to the van and kissed me good-bye. No one on my team had offered to see me off. With perfect symmetry, I left Hungary the same way I arrived after each trip, alone.

April 2000, New York City

Manhattan had become my home away from home. It helped to spend my first few days back at a familiar place to get over jet lag and become oriented. Ever since my parents moved from the East Coast, I had started and ended each trip to the States at an old brownstone in the Upper West side, a former missionary training school for women, called the Hephzibah House.

I boarded an impersonal bus at Kennedy airport, but once I entered the lobby of Hephzibah House, I felt the comfortable surroundings of home.

As before, I woke up with the sun. I grabbed a bagel, coffee, and the New York Times at my favorite corner deli and planted myself on a bench in Central Park to savor the morning. That first day, I had to take care of business. I called my family, got cash and new credit cards, and called my new team to tell them about my latest robbery. I still had two days left to explore the city that never failed to enthrall me.

Things were already looking up. My new team met me at the airport in Orlando. They remembered that would be important to me.

I found an apartment my second day in Orlando, and I moved in on the third day, with only the two suitcases I had been living out of for the last month. Soon after that, my father came, hauling my belongings that had been stored for 10 years. It felt like Christmas opening up those boxes and being reunited with things I had forgotten about or thought were lost forever. Thankfully, the desert air in Arizona protected my photos, but it dried up the glue holding my chairs together. My father re-glued them and clamped them together with vise grips.

I tried to settle in to life in Florida, a new state for me, glad to have the summer before starting my next position with Campus Crusade. Orlando had been a good choice. I already had many friends here, people who had known me for years, and many who had also moved back to the States after living abroad. I lived among people who understood the changes that bombarded me.

I had moved home to a place that no longer felt like home. Knowing that many expatriates are blindsided upon their return, I had tried my best to prepare. It's natural to gear up for life to be different when moving abroad but not to expect coming back "home" to be difficult. I found that home wasn't quite the same as it had been when I left. Moreover, I had changed, and I had different values now.

How could I be unchanged after all I had seen God do? I had known Jesus as my All over there. He held me close to His heart when I felt lonely, protected me, provided everything I needed each day, gave me grace and strength to keep going. I feared that He would not be the same to me in the States, that there might be too many distractions pushing me away, or I'd feel too self-sufficient to need Him as I had.

Like a blind person, I stumbled along unfamiliar paths. I clung to God's promise to lead me in the unknown ways, to make the rough places smooth, and to turn the darkness into light. "God," I cried, "You have sustained me with Your presence, and You've never left me alone. I need You now, once again. I've never traveled this way before."

Returning to the States felt like being in a snow globe that had been shaken, hard. The snow swirled all around me, the waves thrashed, and I thought it would never stop. I felt disoriented much of the time. Like the cartoon characters who burrow through the center of the earth and come up in China, everything seemed upside down.

I had missed an entire decade, the 90s, of the American shared experience. I re-entered a world foreign to me. The volume in restaurants made my head throb, the servers and water-pourers constantly interrupted, the portions were huge, and the prices outrageous. It felt wrong to leave my shoes on when I entered someone's house. Americans now carried water bottles everywhere, as if taking a trek in the desert. People had turned into germaphobes. The toll takers wore latex gloves, and people refused to touch restroom doorknobs, using their elbows instead.

I walked everywhere those first few weeks. I didn't want to lose my European habit of walking, and besides, I didn't have a car yet. When I crossed busy highways in Orlando carrying grocery bags, drivers looked at me as though I had just dropped down from Mars, or worse, as if I was a vagrant. I realized pedestrians are not the norm.

I noticed that my compatriots don't like silence. Between cell phones and earphones, they managed to avoid being alone with their thoughts, instead filling their days with constant noise and activity. I had grown to savor silence to be able to think.

Even in church, I felt out-of-place. I missed the vitality and spontaneity of Eastern European churches. I loved worshipping our same God in each country I used to visit, singing praises to Him in their language. I had been given a taste of what it will be like someday when all the nations gather in heaven to praise the Lamb on His throne, and I wanted more.

Grocery stores stressed me. In May in Florida, the air conditioning felt like January in Siberia. I had grown accustomed to having one kind of milk. Now a dizzying array confronted me: 1%, 2%, skim, fat-free, whole, lactose-free, acidophilus, flavored, goat, organic (coming from cows that were happy), and rice or soy milk that doesn't even come from an animal. I couldn't comprehend the attraction to organic food. In Romania, no pesticides were used, and wormholes dotted the apples, some with worms still inside. If that was organic, I didn't want it.

My friend, Debbie, took me to a Super Wal-Mart to pick up basic supplies. My reverse culture stress came to a head that day. I needed to buy a mop, a broom, and cleaning supplies. When we walked down the aisle with 32 choices of brooms, I felt myself slide into a semi-catatonic state.

"Which one do you want?" Debbie asked.

I stared straight ahead, humming.

"Do you want one of these deluxe brooms?"

I couldn't speak.

"No, of course you don't. You usually pick the cheapest thing. But those look like they might fall apart. Here, let's take this one. It's in the middle. Looks like it'll be sturdy."

I nodded weakly. Debbie made all my choices for me that day because I could not. I was not used to having choices.

The day I bought my used car, I drove to Cocoa Beach, only an hour from Orlando. I needed to be still and regain my equilibrium. I wanted to lean into the sadness, not stunting my experience of grief and having it rear its ugly head later on.

I was homesick for Europe. I missed the old-world grace, the ancientness and beauty, the warmth of the people, the adventure, and even the adrenaline rush. I missed my friends. Leaving had ripped my heart out of my chest, and now I felt numb, afraid I'd never feel again.

I remembered missing America when I lived in Europe. I loved both places and feared I would never feel complete, always longing for the other place. That day, I sat on the warm sand and poured it all out to God. The rhythmic waves mesmerized me, coming and going, in and out. I felt calmed. The magnificence of the ocean soothed my soul.

I remembered sitting on the beach in Spain, just a matter of weeks earlier. It was the same ocean, just the other side of it. Deep within my spirit, God reminded me that He is the same. He created this ocean, and He created me. He understood my churning emotions, even though I could not. His power and beauty and consistency, expressions of His care, spoke to me, assuring me that He'll take the same good care of me in this new home as He always has.

In the midst of the swirling snow, I had found a new place to love, a place that felt strangely right.

June 2000, Harmony, Maryland

I needed to do one more thing before I could start my new role. I wanted to visit my ministry partners to thank them for their part in keeping me in Eastern Europe for a decade, free of worry about finances, confident of their prayer and love for me. They needed to share in the joy of the changed lives as a result of their investment.

I hadn't taken a road trip in years. The drive from Florida to the Eastern Shore of Maryland invigorated me. For two weeks I stayed with friends on the banks of my river, the Choptank.

Once again, the water beckoned to me. Every day, I perched on a wooden swing, held on to the rope handles, and swung.

Out over the edge of the river and back again. I felt secure, as though I had come home.

Since I was a small child, God has called to me from this river, wooing me. I only saw the outer edges of His ways and heard but a faint whisper, but somehow I had recognized His voice.

One day as I swung, I caught my image in the glassiness of the serene river. The reflection that stared back at me was of a little girl, blonde hair and green eyes. I saw myself, 30 years earlier, sitting on a swing my Grandpop made for me, dreaming about being an author. My heart had burst to express itself. I wanted to create, to give back something beautiful to the world, whether through art or music or the written word. The river had given its approval to my childhood dreams all those years before.

As I watched that June day, the river changed in an instant. Clouds darkened the sky, and the wind stirred up choppy white caps, mirroring my tumultuous emotions.

It felt like a moment ago, but somehow 30 years passed. I hadn't pursued my dream, not yet anyway. I knew I hadn't squandered the talent God gave me. My work had been worthwhile. I had invested my life helping others, helping them for eternity. It had been significant, worth the deferment of a dream.

Now I stood on the edge of a new hope, embarking on a new life. That day I understood that, God willing, I had the power to change the course of my future. Time hadn't run out for me to pursue the dream of a little girl on a swing over the Choptank River. That day I promised God that I would write. Now I had something to say. I would write about Eastern Europe, the place that so filled my life that I got lost in it, and about the One who had beckoned me there and kept me there.

I watched the sunlight start again from far off, kissing the other shore. It flirtatiously caught the tips of the waves, winking at me and teasing me to join in its joyous dance of freedom. I felt alive and hopeful. Life will not always be dark and sad. I felt certain that sunlight and dancing waited for me too, maybe around the next corner.

I found myself that day, and I vowed to stay united to the little girl I used to be, holding tightly to her hand.

July 2000, Marin County, California

Before the snow in my globe had settled, it was shaken again. Just when I thought I couldn't possibly handle any more changes, I spent a magical day with my old friend, Steve Hutchison. Two weeks before I arrived in the San Francisco Bay Area to visit my ministry partners there, I became excited, thinking about calling Steve. That came out of nowhere. I hadn't thought about Steve for years.

"Hi, this is Taryn Richardson. Do you remember me?" I asked him over the phone.

"Do I remember you?" he said. "You are unforgettable."

The first day I saw him again, I knew. I hadn't seen him for nine years, since the day I moved my things out of his garage. It had been 14 years since our only date, when I told him I didn't see a future in our relationship because we were headed in different directions. Now it seemed our paths might merge.

We had planned to have lunch but ended up spending all day together. As I drove away, I prayed for Steve, asking God to give him a wife to love him. In the stillness of my heart, I sensed God speaking to me. *I'm doing that. And you're the one.*

The day before, dear friends of mine had mentioned that they knew a wonderful guy they wanted me to meet. I quickly nixed that idea. I had my plate full right now with adjusting to life in Florida. I told them I couldn't possibly handle a romantic relationship with someone in California. This couple didn't know that Steve and I were already friends. If they had mentioned his name, I could have told them I would see him the next day. Instead, they decided to pray and ask God to bring us together. They were certain we'd be perfect for each other.

It surprised me that summer to hear several ministry partners say that they were praying for me to marry. I thought that topic had been laid to rest long ago. I assumed people believed I had moved beyond hope at the age of 43.

Steve held his cards close to his chest that day in July. Always the perfect gentleman, he did nothing to lead me on. I wondered if he felt the same chemistry I had. I didn't know until I arrived home in Orlando. At the office on the first day of my new job, I booted up my computer and found five e-mails waiting for me from Steve.

Our courtship was quick and long-distance. I didn't know how I could emotionally handle more changes, but I was never more convinced of the rightness of a relationship with anyone. Clearly, no person manipulated us getting together. God alone authored it.

I never could get excited about my new position of giving leadership to Stint teams going out all over the world. My heart focused on Steve instead. My first trip took me to Europe for a month to brief several teams starting their year. I met with Eastern European teams in Budapest, Western European teams in Frankfurt, and Middle East teams in Paris. While in Budapest, I tied up a few loose strings and helped my old team with some projects.

Soon after I returned from Europe, Steve came to visit me in Orlando. We celebrated our mutual birthday together. During those few days, I fell in love with his tender heart, his confidence and positive spirit, his loyalty and dependability. I admired his discipline in prayer and exercise. His dashing good looks sure didn't hurt either. I saw that Steve had healed from his divorce all those years ago, being set free from bitterness, free to marry again.

Early in December, I traveled to Chile to help set up a future project there. The day we were scheduled to leave, my team of nine waited at a café in Santiago. Our carry-on luggage sat underneath our table. At least five of our group were always at the table.

While I visited the restroom, someone grabbed my bag and slipped out, bringing my total to five robberies in five years. I remembered my altruistic feelings when my camera had been stolen on the train to Slovenia, glad it hadn't happened to the national women. This time was different. *Why didn't the thieves take someone else's bag? I'm tired of it always being mine.*

I couldn't take out my contact lenses before the flight, since my glasses were stolen. I had no book to read or sweater to wear, and I'd lost another camera. The biggest loss was my journal. I had recorded all the minute details of my courtship with Steve, and now it was gone. I hoped I could re-create it, but the memories would never be as fresh.

The flight to Miami lasted all night. I sat in the middle of three seats. Two smelly, overweight men on either side of me snored with their heads on my shoulders. Those hours were some of the most miserable of my life.

Upon deplaning in Miami, I discovered that my flight to Orlando had been delayed several more hours. When I finally arrived home, my contacts were stuck to my eyes, and my frustration level had reached new heights. I called Steve to vent about what I had endured.

Steve listened, belting out his hearty laugh, which I usually loved, as I described the two men on the plane. Like any good engineer, he tried to fix things. He wanted to help me feel better. He told me over the phone, "You'd better get some sleep so you'll be more rational."

"You haven't seen irrational yet," I said. Still, I agreed to visit him for the holidays.

I arrived in the Bay Area 10 days before Christmas, still fuming about his insensitivity after this last robbery. It didn't take long for sweet Steve to win me over. He whipped up feasts that we savored in front of a crackling fire. As we walked hand-in-hand through the hills, he told me he liked to sit on the patio in the evenings and listen to crickets chirping—he wasn't driven by work or tied to computers or technical gadgets like most American guys I knew. *I could marry someone like this.*

Steve took me Christmas caroling at San Quentin State Prison, the place where he had witnessed lives being changed for years now. He wanted me to meet two inmates who had been praying for me. When we entered their cell block, Steve yelled up to them on the fifth tier.

"Terrance! Energy! Here she is!"

We discussed the last few issues that we needed to talk through before we were ready. My heart had wanted to marry Steve back in July. My mind needed to catch up. I expected mixed-up emotions with culture stress, and I had to be sure I wasn't subconsciously trying to escape my world being turned inside out. Now I could say with confidence that God intended for Steve and me to be together.

On the day of the winter solstice, December 21—the darkest day of the year but one of the brightest of my life—Steve Hutchison got down on one knee and read me beautiful words he had penned. If he hadn't written them down, I would never remember what he said that day. I did, however, catch the question at the end loud and clear. "Will you marry me?"

I quickly answered, "Yes, I will be honored to be your wife." A few hours later, I met his college-age children, Kyle and Lisa. They welcomed me to the family, relieved that their dad would no longer be alone. Steve and I picked out a platinum engagement ring that reminded me of my grandmother's, but that means so much more to me than the one I lost.

Steve and me celebrating our engagement.

I experienced God's truth that there is a time for everything. I had my time to weep, to mourn, and to be uprooted. Now a new season unfolded before me, and it involved laughing, dancing, and planting deep roots.

My mind and heart had never connected with my job in Orlando, instead being pulled toward leaving and preparing to cleave to my fiancé. I coordinated a huge conference in Thailand for Stinters serving in Central Asia, just six weeks before my wedding. I found it hard to focus. Besides, I came down with a terrible case of bronchitis due to the pollution in Thailand. The results of my work didn't meet up to the quality my director and I hoped to achieve. I had wanted to leave Campus Crusade on a high note, not this disappointment of a mediocre final project.

In spite of my illness, I did find time to have my wedding dress created by an Indian seamstress in Thailand. The sign on her shop door read, "Suits—24 hours—$100." When I asked if she could make a wedding dress, she agreed. It took 48 hours and cost $150. The dress, made of Chinese silk, vaguely resembled the drawing I'd made. I tried it on for the fitting before the sleeves had been attached. When I took it home, I found I couldn't move my arms. They were stuck in position to carry a bouquet in front of me. I foresaw problems with lifting my arms to kiss Steve or with throwing the bouquet. I figured I could drop-kick it. Back in Florida, a Cuban tailor fixed the arms somewhat, and an American woman of German heritage added beads to make it prettier. It took the world to make my wedding dress.

Tacking on long-distance wedding planning proved to be too much with everything else. I had to wrap up 21 years with Campus Crusade, my only job since college. Campus Crusade had been my family, much more than a career, and I had to say good-bye to many dear friends. Once again, I found myself packing and moving.

I begged Steve for a simple wedding with only our immediate families. I told him if we had an elaborate one, the white I'd wear would be my strait jacket and my attendants would be the ones who'd carry me out in a stretcher afterward. He relented.

We planned a romantic elopement. Since we told everyone the date ahead of time, and Steve didn't carry me off on a ladder in the middle of the night, I guess we didn't exactly elope. Instead, we had an intimate ceremony without stressful details. We chose a small church at Lake Tahoe and invited our closest family to come.

The sun smiled over the blue lake that March 31st. Our wedding day was perfect and the ceremony meaningful. Winter had passed. The turtledoves warmed up their voices, and the buds prepared to open.

April 2001, Marin County, California

Four weeks later, exactly one year after I returned to the States, we invited our friends to come to our reenactment reception. We wore our tux and gown and repeated the vows we had written for each other. It was another stress-free day. It's much easier to have a wedding when you're already married.

By the time my first year back in the States had ended, I had moved twice, made two career changes, and gotten married, even inheriting two adult stepchildren. Life with my even-keeled husband proved to be the easiest adjustment of all, certainly the most fun. I threw my cross-cultural adjustments a curve by adding so many extra transitions. The snow in my globe continued to swirl.

Usually, change invigorates me. I think I overdid it this time. Everything in my life was different. Even my name changed. I felt as if I'd joined the Witness Protection Plan. I had been given a new name, a new identity, and been concealed deep undercover to make it as difficult as possible for people from my past to find me.

I tested myself according to the Social Readjustment Rating Scale, the one that lists major life changes, assigning each a point value. A score over 300 is bad news because of the negative impact stress causes. My score during that 12-month period totaled 429, which didn't include some bonus points I think I deserved. The test gives a move across town the same number of points as the kind of relocations I made. My moves from one country to another, and then one side of the States to another, should have given me extra credit.

Impatient to feel at home in my new life, I poured out my insecurities to the Lord. I sensed Jesus gently whisper to me,

213

Honey, you are at home. Your home is with Me. I live in your heart, and I'll never leave you.

I had been afraid that Jesus wouldn't be the same for me in the States, that I wouldn't need Him as I had overseas. Instead, I found He is still the Lover of my soul, even though I have an earthly husband now. He has not stopped taking good care of me.

The one familiar part of my new life is the most important thing. My Rock has not changed. I waited on Him, and He proved Himself faithful. He guided me on the unfamiliar paths, leading me to Eastern Europe and back again. I had come home with Him.

What About You?

- How do you define home? Where is that for you?

- How do you deal with stress and change? Even good changes that you choose bring stress, but sometimes change is forced upon us against our will. How do you regain your equilibrium?

- Which season are you in—the one to laugh or the one to weep—and why?

- Have you ever taken a whole day to spend alone with the Lord? If you can, go out to a pretty spot in nature with a journal and your Bible. Be still and listen for His voice. What do you sense Him speaking to you? Make a list of the times God has met you and you've seen evidence of His provision of grace and strength. Offer Him your hopes and dreams for the future.

EPILOGUE: GLORY IN THE MUNDANE

"I will rejoice in doing them good and will assuredly plant them in this land with all my heart and soul."

—Jeremiah 32:41 (NIV)

October 2005, Marin County, California

NOW THAT I'VE had a few years to settle in to my new life, I find that it's really not all that different from my former one. I'm still the same person with the same issues, the same bent to protect myself, the same self-centeredness. As I'd expected, marriage didn't bring an end to my problems. The big difference, which really is huge, is that now I have my best friend to walk with through life. I don't have to make decisions and shoulder everything alone.

Even with the companionship that marriage brings, I still struggle with loneliness. There aren't many women who can identify with me getting married for the first time in my forties and inheriting adult stepchildren when I never had children of my own. And when I add having worked in ministry for over 20 years and having lived overseas for 10 years, I doubt anyone exists like me. As before, I've learned to make a composite best girlfriend from several people, near and far, letting them share the role and fulfill different needs in my life.

My routine administrative job at Golden Gate Seminary doesn't get my blood pumping, and it might even be described as mundane. I do enjoy the open door it gives me to build mentoring relationships with students, slightly older than college students, with hearts for the lost to know Christ. I understand the big picture. I'm not just making a cog to put in a spaceship, but I'm helping to send people to the moon (or in this case, China or Africa). At times, I feel overlooked, and I wonder if anyone knows what I'm capable of doing, but usually I'm happy for a simpler job so I can focus my time and energy on writing and being a good wife for Steve.

Living in Marin County has proved to be a bigger hurdle than I'd counted on. I couldn't have chosen a place more radically different in lifestyle and values from Eastern Europe if I'd tried. While Eastern Europeans are characterized as warm, generous, and humble, Marinites might be described as proud, elitist, and self-absorbed. They also happen to be some of the wealthiest, and loneliest, people on the planet.

I need to trust God to fill my heart with love for these prickly people I live among, just as He did on the foreign mission field. I'm ashamed to admit my attitude sometimes begs for realignment. I want to see them with God's eyes of compassion, as people He created and dearly loves. They have the same needs as impoverished Romanians and people anywhere. They need to be loved, and they need a Savior. They just happen to be so skilled at covering over their deficiencies and anesthetizing the pain, they often are oblivious to it themselves. This gorgeous county on San Francisco Bay is the geography where God has called me and planted me for now—that is, until the cloud moves and He leads Steve and me elsewhere.

Before I could complete my adjustment back to life in the States, I needed to return to Eastern Europe and have my two worlds connect with each other. The trip I took with my husband, flying to Hungary and taking the train to Romania and several other of my countries, was a necessary part of the process. I had to know that in my attempt to feel at home again in the land of my birth, I hadn't lost the place that captured my heart and is embedded deep within.

Steve and me back home at the Blue Danube in Budapest.

There is nothing dramatic in my life now, and usually I'm thankful to be able to breathe again. I'm learning to submit my plans each day to God's agenda, letting Him make me into a blessing for the people whose paths intersect mine that day, letting Him bring meaning out of the mundane. I have learned that I can't minister to others out of a hollow vacuum any better on this side of the ocean; I need to be filled up by God first so I can spill out. If I can't be kind to the cashier in my check-out line, then it doesn't matter what glorious wonders I've been part of in the past. It's in the hidden moments that my true nature is revealed.

What God asks of me is to yield each day to Him, whether I plan to spend it at home doing laundry or entering tedious data in a computer. As morning breaks, I offer it to God, saying, "Lord, I want to do, to be, and to say only what You want for me this day that You've given to me." I imagine myself laying my head on His chest and listening to His heart beat for me and for the world He created, people who will never be complete until they know their Maker.

Steve and I start every morning reading from the devotional *My Utmost for His Highest.* Oswald Chambers often spoke about the superb grace of God displayed in drudgery. He wrote, "It requires the inspiration of God to go thru drudgery with the light of God upon it.…The tendency is to look for the marvellous in our experience; we mistake the sense of the heroic for being heroes. It is one thing to go through a crisis grandly, but another thing to go through every day glorifying God when there is no witness, no limelight, no one paying the remotest attention to us."

God continues to protect me and provide for me, giving me enough grace and strength to live as He wants and to do what He has given me to do. He enables me to perform my daily routine with a smile (at least most days), showing a glimmer of His light. It's not natural for me, but I have found it's possible with His help to do mundane tasks with an attitude of thankfulness, as though I'm working for Him. That glorifies Him.

We can reflect His image from any place, doing anything. The things I experienced in Eastern Europe, while more exciting, are no more significant than what I face now. God has called me to this new season of my life. He is faithful. He will enable me to live it, and He will enable you, too. We can depend on Him to bring it to pass.

Countless times, people in Eastern Europe said to me, "We wait you. Long time." I ask you, who waits for you?

As they say in Romania,

"Happy End."

What About You?

- Does your daily routine ever feel like drudgery? In what ways?

- How can you yield each day to God and try to do your work as though you're working for Him?

- Try to think of the place God has put you as your mission field. What will change in your attitude? Priorities? Schedule? What steps can you take to get to know and care about the people you live among?

- How can you trust God to enable you to do whatever He's given you to do, wherever you happen to be?

ABOUT THE AUTHOR

TARYN R. HUTCHISON has published several short stories and articles, but this is her debut book. She hails from a town on the Eastern Shore of Maryland with a booming population of 75 people, three million chickens, and several dogs. Taryn loves people, art, storytelling, and travel. She's visited all 50 states, lots of countries, and every continent except Antarctica—having lived all over the U.S. and even Romania and Hungary. She prefers the real local culture to a tourist resort any day. Taryn served on staff with Campus Crusade for Christ for 21 years, later working at Golden Gate Seminary. She and her husband recently relocated from the bustling San Francisco Bay area to a sleepy town in western North Carolina.

You can continue your experience with *We Wait You*, share your thoughts and communicate with Taryn. Visit her website at **www.tarynhutchison.com** and her blog at **tarynhutchison. authorweblog.com**.

PW

CPSIA information can be obtained at www.ICGtesting.com
Printed in the USA
LVOW102030050412

276329LV00002B/4/P